Write
Like You Talk
Only Better

The secret to pulling ideas out of your head and onto the page

Barb Sawyers

D0814399

DEDICATION

To all the people who want to make more of themselves and
their world through writing

CONTENTS

ACKNOWLEDGMENTS

Many thanks to my daughter Maddy for goof proofing;
Lee Weisser for listening; Mary Ann Cattral for her
discerning eye; Lucia Kuzminski for insight on positioning;
Amy Sept for the keen editing as well as Liza Magcale, Jim
Pagiamtzis and other test readers for the honest sharing
that took me from hugging trees to embracing the forest.

1 LOOK IN THE MIRROR

I'll bet you've looked in the mirror and said to yourself:
"I can be more than this."

That happened to me when I turned 50. Sure, I had
reached some of my life objectives, such as amazing kids, a
nice house and loyal clients.

But there was more I wanted to do, more I wanted to
become. I had only 50 more years to do it. Yikes!

It wasn't about crossing exotic destinations off my bucket
list. It was about seeing what I, the one and only Barb
Sawyers, could do.

I couldn't say I was too busy with my kids, now teens.
Nor could I blame my stagnation on my parents' low
expectations, my ex-husband's betrayal, obsessive media
consumption, chocolate, vulnerable interest rates or a full
dishwasher.

It was up to me.

I wanted to help people, but not by holding cold cloths
on hot foreheads in refugee camps or mapping seating plans
for charity galas.

No, I wanted to help all the poor people who were chained to their computers, cranking out emails, reports, dating profiles, posts and other written communication. What's more, I wanted to help all the people stuck reading that stuff.

I wanted to help people like Deanne Kelleher, founder and director of Kaos Group. A professional organizer, Deanne loves sharing her passion for imposing order on chaos, from transforming crowded cupboards to streamlining digital files.

After a long day of making lists with clients, taking her kids to swimming lessons and struggling to meet the deadline for her monthly online magazine, she decided to rest her eyes—just for five minutes. The next morning little Tess found her slumped over, asleep at her desk.

Deanne vowed to change. She could not stomach missing a deadline. She hated the example she had set for her kids. She was desperate to balance her work with time to play with her children, fiancé and friends. But how?

She could hire a professional, but only a psychic ghost writer would be able to pull those ideas out of her head and save all that much time.

Deanne figured she should be able to find an organized approach for writing her magazine, blog and the other marketing material she relied on to attract a steady stream of customers.

I met Deanne when she was one of the facilitators at a small-business coaching group. The leaders kept telling us to focus on what we do best and outsource the rest. But like Deanne, they insisted on doing most of their own writing. They wanted to pull out and share all those great thoughts going to waste in their heads.

Deanne became my most enthusiastic test reader for the first edition of *Write Like You Talk—Only Better*. As soon as she realized the book would help her write more efficiently and effectively, the color-coded highlighting began.

She is still using the checklists and worksheets for *Organized Lifestyle Magazine* and other writing. Through this practice, she's keeping up with her writing without falling asleep at her desk. Better still, Deanne is capturing the sugared-up Martha Stewart that people love in her live and televised presentations.

This book worked for Deanne; it can work for you too.

In a world where you communicate so much online, where you need to stand out to be heard, writing is a means to many ends.

Writing to connect with more people can help you follow your dreams. When you look in the mirror, you'll be happier with your reflection.

Knowing I've helped, I'll feel better about my reflection too, though you can bet I'll still bitch about my failure to lose ten pounds.

So read this book. And give yourself one more reason to look in the mirror and say "Wow!"

> Pull those ideas out of your head and onto the page.

2 GO FOR RESULTS

It's not them—it's you

Maybe it's emails, tweets or collaborations at work; Facebook, texts and messaging the rest of the time. Chances are you write a lot.

If you are a digital native, you probably take it for granted that much of your communication is written, not spoken. You probably use your cell phone more for texting than talking.

Despite how important and time-consuming your writing is, it may not accomplish what you want.

Perhaps people aren't showing up prepared for your meetings. They aren't grabbing on to your ideas. They aren't buying your products. They aren't responding to your dating profile. They aren't giving you a job interview. They aren't voting for your idea. They aren't telling their friends. They aren't doing what you want them to.

Maybe you recognize yourself in some of these scenarios:

Lauren loves writing. Too bad she doesn't show the love to her readers by thinking about their interests, terminology and time. That's why her love is so often unrequited.

Cecil thinks he shows respect and a business-appropriate demeanor by peppering his emails with hollow formalities

4

such as "as per your request" and "warmest regards." But people don't warm up to him.

Mel is so used to writing/chatting spontaneously online that she neglects all the planning, improving, tightening and other thinking that would take her essays and posts to the next level.

Li produces lots of white papers, but nobody seems to remember what's in them. Most people don't remember Li either.

Maria, BS, MBA, PhD, uses long words and sentences, many pages and lots of capital letters. Despite her obvious brains, she can't entice people to read through her content. But how else can she become a thought leader?

Asif relies so heavily on spell check to find his mistakes that he often confuses sound-alike words, especially "it's" and "its." This makes his supervisor think he's sloppy and confuses others. Too bad, because he deserves a better job.

Ethan churns out number-filled reports about how well his sales team is doing. After all, he's busy and it's not a movie script. But the executives are not giving him the credit he craves.

Sound familiar? Each of these people would progress faster and farther in their quest for success if only they could download a serious writing-skills update. But instead of tech short cuts, it will take brain work for Lauren, Cecil, Mel, Li, Maria, Asif and Ethan to upgrade their writing. You too. Fortunately, pretty much everything you need to learn is in this book.

Don't blame your readers for not taking the time or being smart enough to get you. Don't fall for those no-work Internet success pitches. Take responsibility.

How to use this book

Writing is a skill you need to achieve your results. However, it's not magic. By going back to your first and favorite way to communicate, talking, you will remember the basics. By reading this book and practicing, you'll learn how to avoid writer's block and recall the few grammar rules that still matter. You'll progress to the next level.

In my 30 years as a writer and editor, I've seen lots of reasons why people aren't able to use writing to get more of what they want out of life. But instead of patching over the same old weak spots, I decided to write a book that would help people overcome common problems and produce results.

Although I borrow techniques from the novelists, screen writers, lyricists, comedians and other artists I admire, I'm not talking about creative writing. I'm talking about the practical writing you do every day.

You are busy, I know. So I don't expect you to comb through every page or complete every exercise. Skim through this book once, then return to the sections where you see yourself. Read those sections again.

The next time you have something important to write practice with the worksheets and checklists at the end. Keep working with them until writing becomes as natural as talking.

The cellulite will disappear, hair on your head will reappear, you'll lose the fear, won't run out of beer... Okay, I'm exaggerating, a little.

But I do guarantee that writing will become easier, faster and, yes, even enjoyable. You'll connect with the people who matter most, attract like-minded people and build a community.

All without returning to those boring high school grammar classes. Instead, you'll go back to the fun roots of communication—talking.

Why talking counts

Talking is the first way you learned to communicate. By talking, you grasped the fundamentals of engaging communication long before you learned how to write.

Talking is likely still your favorite way to connect with your nearest and dearest. Even in an era where we communicate through writing more and more, talking rules.

Consider these examples. You talk to your team when the news really matters. You work up to talking to the person you met on the dating site. You close big sales through in-person conversation.

When you're writing and forget the correct way to phrase something, you go back to what sounds right.

It's so frustrating when people write when they should talk. Think about how wounded you feel when a friend texts to cancel a date. Or how you pull out your hair when the call center rep reads a script instead of answering your question. Or how you yawn when the presenter reads from the slides or teleprompter.

Why can't they just talk to you?

They should. But frequently, you cannot talk individually to everyone who matters. But you *can* capture more of the intimacy of live conversation by writing like you talk.

Plus, as Seth Godin said, "Nobody gets talker's block."

When I was studying French, I knew I was getting somewhere when conversation started to come naturally. A little wine and a cute guy from Quebec helped.

I never reached that level in German. I am still stunned when I hear people speak it. How can conversation flow when they need to think about all those fiddly rules?

Of course, Germans don't think about the rules, just as we converse without thinking about English grammar. We simply talk.

When people talk, they go from mind to mouth. But when they write, many jump from mind to mouse. By skipping the mouth, they shut out their intuitive grasp of the rules and the social nature of conversation.

When you write like you talk, you go from mind to mouth to mouse. Suddenly all that writing you do is easier and friendlier.

Maybe writing will never become as automatic and fun as talking. After all, you're not simply transcribing chatter. You are thinking more.

By thinking before you write, you won't miss the point, piss off people or go on for too long. By thinking after you write, you can make sure you look good, respect people's time and maybe even add some magic.

Combine the warmth and spontaneity of talking with the thought and reach of writing and you'll soon start to see better results. That is the secret to pulling those ideas out of your head and onto the page.

The writing road trip

Writing is like a road trip. You study the maps and tourist information to plan. You hit the road.

You return home, taking a faster or more scenic route.

If you take the same trip again, it could be even better. You'll pay less attention to the directions from A to B and more to enjoying the ride. Maybe you'll travel farther.

1. Plan

Effective writing starts with thinking about who you want to connect with, what you're going to say and how you're going to say it.

This gives writing a great advantage over talking, as I'm reminded every time I blurt out something insensitive. Although you may spend a little more time at the outset, these minutes can save lots more time later.

It's like studying the maps and reviewing the tourist information before you head out on a road trip. It will keep you from getting lost or missing the most stunning sights.

2. Write like you talk

This means more than writing in a conversational style. It's also about writing freely, like hitting the open road when you know where you're going and the sun is shining. It's the free flow of conversation combined with the creative surge of writing. This is the most fun.

3. Make it better

You'll chop the length so it's faster for readers and more focused on what you want to say. You'll broaden the lens to include other important people.

You'll hack out the biggest, baddest grammar mistakes, punctuation excesses and other problems that can cloud your meaning.

4. Reach the next level

You'll take your writing to new levels by applying advanced techniques from movies, music and other media. You'll go farther faster.

5. Practice

Like driving, the more writing you do, the better you will become. That's why I've concluded with worksheets and checklists you can keep on applying until everything comes naturally.

With practice, you'll get more of the results you desire. Just as handling curves and shifting gears become automatic for the experienced driver, so will writing that connects become natural for you.

In the next chapters, you'll explore the three questions that will create your road map.

Who do I most want to connect with? What is my point? What's my best way to make it?

3 WHO DO YOU WANT TO CONNECT WITH?

It's all about them

Maybe you're writing an email to the members of your team. Although your main point may be the meeting you want them to attend, you need to think about how they feel about your meetings, the topic you're going to discuss and other concerns.

Taking the time to consider their perspectives can allow you to highlight the benefits for them, overcome their objections or maybe even excite them. The result could be not only better attendance, but also less checking of smartphones and a well-informed and enthusiastic discussion.

Better still, think of the one person you'd most like to connect with. Chances are you can take for granted the keeners who always show up, prepared and psyched. You know better than to waste your effort on that troll who plots your demise. Likely you'll want to appeal to that person who is sitting on the fence, ready to jump to your side with a little encouragement.

Think of that person while you're writing and you'll attract like-minded people too.

Writing for your ideal readers should also encourage you to avoid the jargon of your business, company or profession. If you are writing to someone in your own specialty, some technical terms may provide a convenient shorthand. Occasionally it's wise to speak in your target reader's dialect. Take the example of a resume for an IT position with a highly technical job description.

But if you have any doubts about whether your ideal reader will fully understand a word, opt for plain language that everyone will understand.

People rattle off emails so quickly that they often neglect this important step. Or they write proposals, thinking more of how their boss will react than the end reader. But if you try this approach, you'll quickly see how a brief investment of thought can produce an impressive return. You will also avoid coming off like that self-centered talker you routinely tune out.

If you're writing for people you don't know personally, you'll need to combine insight and imagination to get psyched about the fantasy person you'd most like to connect with.

More on that later in this chapter. First, let me show you how I do it.

My ideal reader

You, my ideal reader, want all your writing to become easier and faster. You don't want to relearn all those boring grammar rules, though you'd be embarrassed if you made mistakes that made you look unprofessional.

You have some expertise or information that's worth sharing.

You want people to pay attention, remember and take a specific action. You want people to "Like" you and really like you.

I've asked the two most important questions: What gets you out of bed in the morning? What keeps you up at night?

You are on a mission to help people become more organized, at home or work, so they'll have time for what's truly important in life. You lose sleep worrying about keeping up with your own big fat life, terrified that people will catch you in a messy moment.

Now what about yours?

Your ideal reader

If you're communicating to other people at work, you probably know a lot about them.

If you're selling a product or service, you likely have a pretty clear idea of your ideal customer. Or at least you should.

Your ideal reader may be more specific than your ideal customer. She's the one who will not only skim your post, but give it the attention it deserves.

You need to know this ideal reader as well as you can because you are going to pretend you two are talking.

But how, my ideal reader might ask, do you do that when you're writing for strangers?

If you know some people in the group you're writing for, pick the person you most want to influence and pretend you're talking.

If you're writing for a large group, potentially the world when you write for the web, pretend you're chatting with just one person, the kind of person you expect would most enjoy, jump to your side or otherwise benefit from what you're writing about. Visualize one with a tight tush, a dragon tattoo, deep pockets or whatever else motivates you.

As with your ideal customer, you need to know all about gender, age, education, income and other demographic factors. But don't stop there.

Imagine pains and problems, pastimes and passions. What keeps your ideal reader up at night? What makes your ideal reader jump for joy? What makes him weep? What makes her pull out her credit card?

Frequently people make decisions based on subconscious feelings, like the desire to look good in front of their peers. So spend some time exploring the heart and mind of your ideal reader. Or think about the inner workings of real people you know well who are similar in some ways to your ideal reader.

You may also want to consider some communication from the kind of person you most want to connect with. This will help make sure your writing style is in tune with theirs. Using a Google search-like algorithm, James Pennebaker studied language people used in online dating profiles. People whose profiles used similar pronouns, articles and other parts of speech were most likely to end up together, he found. This and other research and insight in his book, *The Secret Life of Pronouns*, tells me that compatible language styles will help you attract customers and other important people too.

Unless your ideal reader writes in an authentic voice, however, I would lean more toward examining their spoken communication.

Often people will say they are writing for everyone or a long list of so-called stakeholders. But that can mean they're connecting to no one, like they're shouting to the entire cocktail party instead of picking someone attractive and striking up a conversation.

Sure, you may have other audiences or stakeholders that you need to consider. But to deeply connect, you need to focus on one specific reader. Later, when you're following my advice on making your writing better, you can add content for the other people who are important to you.

Your understanding of your ideal reader will also help you choose your most appropriate approach, for example whether you should appeal mainly to emotions or logic. What's more, you can employ the terminology, examples, humor, questions and other elements that your ideal reader will understand, relate to and enjoy.

When you think about your ideal reader, you'll also consider how you want this person to feel, act and think. Do you want them to feel good about themselves, buy your product or shrink their carbon footprint?

Don't limit yourself to obvious, outward actions. Also significant are symbolic gestures, like inspiring your readers to consider the water wasted when they brush their teeth.

Remember you are courting your ideal reader, starting with attraction then building understanding and respect. Expecting your ideal reader to immediately buy your product or otherwise commit may be unrealistic. Then again, never rule out love at first sight or Romeo and Juliet living happily ever after.

For a worksheet you can fill in about your ideal reader, see page 88.

You too

Because conversations involve you too, you need to think about how you're going to express your personality in writing. Marketing folks like to call this your brand.

Are you funny? Are you known for uncovering obscure research in your specialty? Perhaps people remember your pet expression, like Barney Flintstone's "Ya-ba-da-ba-doo" or Paris Hilton's "That's hot."

Do you have values or experience, such as a passion for helping children or playing basketball, that will help you bond with your ideal reader?

For some people, it's difficult to write as a human being. Formal writing allows them to erect a barrier that protects them from their reader. Like phoniness and small talk, this precludes any intimacy.

But without intimacy, there is little connection, conversation or conversion. That means fewer people attending your event, signing up for your newsletter or being excited to work at your company.

Maybe you are writing for somebody else or on behalf of an organization. This makes sociability more difficult, but not impossible. Much as an actor would do, you have to slip into the personality of the person or organization you're writing for.

Although it's ideal to know the person you're writing for well, often you're fronting for a busy person who has little time for you.

That was the challenge when I wrote speeches for politicians. Usually, the bosses would give me the talking points, easy to write. But if I wanted to bring those points to life, and have the audience cheering, I needed to work with the politician's personality.

So I would watch him in debates on cable television and in live meetings. I would notice what made him smile and what pissed him off, as well as his speech patterns and favorite expressions.

In my imagination, I would fill in some gaps with characteristics that would make the politician an appealing human being, such as self-deprecating humor or passion for a cause dear to his party.

When I sat down to write, I would channel the spirit of the politician. I would anticipate and respond to the audience's questions and objections. I would build in pauses for the audience to react to his jokes or emotional punches. I would not write the concluding "thank you" until I knew the audience was pumped for a standing ovation.

Of course my brilliant oratory sometimes didn't make the podium, what with bureaucrats and lawyers downgrading my Cadillac to a Pontiac. But because I had aimed high, I didn't end up with a Pinto, the car blamed for deathly explosions in the 1970s.

Many people produce white papers, reports and other content for a faceless organization. So they need to create a personality for the company, often integrating a few of their own characteristics.

Fortunately, you can usually learn a lot about an organization's personality in corporate values, brand promises and mission statements.

Still, you have to use your imagination to flesh out a personality from those elements. Rather than repeating corporate platitudes, you need to probe deeply into the corporate psyche, asking yourself what would make this person get out of bed in the morning and what would keep her up at night.

When I ask participants to create this personality during a workshop, they always come up with fresh and personal ways to create a face for their organization. Give it a shot.

You need two personalities, the reader and the writer, to have a conversation. While conveying the personality of the person or organization you're writing for is important, don't forget to keep the focus on the people who will be reading or listening.

It's like spotting a person you'd like to get to know at a networking event. You don't talk much about yourself. You ask that person about themselves. After all, it's all about them, for starters anyways.

For a worksheet on how to convey your personality or the personality of the person or organization you're writing for, go to page 90.

> Connect with one
> Attract many
> Build community

4 WHAT'S YOUR POINT?

Before you hit the keyboard you need to have a concise, focused message, expressed in about 25 words. Likely, but not necessarily, it will encompass the who, what, when, where and why as well as the key benefits. That's a lot to ask of 25 words.

Don't worry if your message starts off longer. But keep shortening until you have reached a point of clarity.

The fewer the words, the sharper your focus. And the more likely you are to pierce through the clutter of thoughts and competition of ideas.

Some well-educated people would argue they are dumbing down their writing when they simplify. Wrong, wrong, wrong.

Being able to clearly summarize your point in 25 words or less demonstrates just how well you understand it and how clearly you think. Neuroscientists, such as Dr. Norman Doidge who wrote *The Brain That Changes Itself,* have found that the ability to summarize is actually a left-hemisphere symbolic thinking activity that can improve with practice.

Longer explanations are of course necessary for complex ideas, but they will come later. You need to start with one highly focused message.

17

Writing is not exploring the cosmos. It's more like splitting the atom. The smaller, the more powerful.

With shorter attention spans and the limits of Twitter and texting, the skill to distill is becoming ever more valuable.

This may take several drafts. During this stage, the elegance of your language is not important. The sharpness of your focus is.

Once you've crafted your main point, relate it to your ideal reader. Does it fit?

Then tie your main point to the objective you want to achieve.

To draft your point, use the worksheet on page 91.

My point is to help people fulfill their potential by connecting with others through friendlier, smarter writing. What's yours?

5 HOW TO MAKE YOUR POINT

The structure is the road that will take you to your destination, the results you want to achieve.

When you start writing, you will introduce your point and summarize how you're going to make it. In the body, you'll expand through this structure. You'll link it to your route and objectives at the end. You can get a lot of mileage out of the right structure.

For now, though, let's focus on selecting the structure that will help you best achieve your objectives. Because this compels you to think through how you're going to write, it's your best guarantee against writer's block. This logical framework will also help your readers understand and remember what you've written.

Your basic practical choices are: inform, instruct, advise, persuade or inspire.

Feel free to mix and match, especially if you're writing something long or complex. For example, I'm using a step-by-step order common to books intended to instruct. I've also organized some of the sections as tips. And of course I want to persuade you to tell others to buy this book.

Inform

Although there's usually a persuasive element, practical writing often leans heavily toward providing information.

If you are telling your readers what's new, start with that, working backwards from the most important news to the least important background. This is the classic inverted pyramid style I learned in journalism school. Use your ideal reader's pains and passions to help you prioritize.

There are many others ways to organize your information. The point is to pick the most appropriate organizational framework. For example, if you are writing a report on your department's monthly sales, you could organize your information

• by region
• by product or service
• from top to bottom sales or bottom to top
• under an acronym, e.g. GRIP (growth retention invoices profit)

You can use your organizational structure to help your readers scan your document through

• subheads
• bullet points
• numbered points

You can reinforce these points through graphs and other visuals. You could also:

• compare the new to the known, i.e. this month to last month, your new product to what consumers now use
• explain how it fits into the bigger picture, i.e. the competitive environment or the organization's strategic plan
• emphasize how the information will affect the individuals you expect will be reading the report.

Instruct

If your objective is to explain how to do something, as in manuals, recipes or processes:

• Start with anything the reader needs to do or have in advance. For example, recipes first list the ingredients, the oven preheat temperature and any special equipment.

• Use numbered steps dished out in chronological order.

• Explain each step separately, clearly explaining and deleting any unnecessary or unhelpful wording, but repeating any vital points as needed.

• Add simple illustrations or video links to help readers see what to do or check that they are correctly following your instructions.

• Remember that your readers will likely refer back to the instructions. So make them easy to review, with subheads, diagrams, indexes or helpful signs and reminders.

Advise

When you're instructing readers on, say, how to install a dishwasher, you can't skip any steps. In contrast, when you're advising on what to look for in a dishwasher, you're writing about only what's important.

To provide advice, offer tips:

1. with numbered points
2. limited to no more than five; three are even easier to understand and remember
3. that start with the most important and finish with the second most important point.

Although a popular blogging technique, this approach has been around for a long time. Who hasn't been intrigued by those covers of *Cosmopolitan* magazine promising *5 Ways to Tell if Your Man is Cheating*?

Unlike informing, advising should not involve a long list, so keep your advice short and focused. If you have lots of points to cover, consider breaking them into separate posts or other content modules.

For example, with this book, I've sprinkled the advice in many different sections. It would have been a quicker read if I'd called it *100 Tips to Rev up Your Writing*. But you probably would not have read or remembered much.

People reading yet another post called *100 Tips for SEO Success* will likely recall only the few tips that are most relevant to them. The same goes for the people who read your emails, reports and proposals. Keep it brief so it's easy for them to understand and focus on your wise counsel.

Persuade

If writing to persuade people were all that easy, I would be a billionaire. And I would write notes to remind my teens to clean up after themselves.

But writing to persuade takes time and motivation.

Like you, I need to build awareness and credibility and convince readers that I can solve their problem or meet a need. To do that, I have to answer the reader's question: what's in it for me?

Personal benefits

The benefit to you from reading this book is advice that will make your writing easier and achieve your goals. With my teens, it usually involves money or favors.

Whether you're selling a product or pursuing a more subtle goal like building respect for your expertise, you need to focus on benefits for others. That means whatever you're writing, from post to presentation, has to be more about the reader or audience and less about you and your product, service or expertise.

You have to back up the benefits through emotions and logic. The balance will depend on the people you're appealing to and the specifics of your objective.

For example, people will give more to charity if the plea tells a poignant story than if it provides statistics, alarming though they may be. In contrast, your business case has to rationally explain how your great idea will make or save money.

Start with the needs and desires of your ideal reader to determine the balance of heart and mind. For example, someone selling allergy-sensitive cleaning products to families should stress the emotional and physical health benefits over the science. On the other hand, if you're selling apps to geeks, focus on how they work.

However, even if you are taking a mostly logical approach, you need to touch some of the emotions that motivate everyone, curmudgeons included. Similarly, warm emotional appeals often need to be backed up by proven facts.

Hearts

To understand what motivates people, you need to drill down to the emotions that drive them. Fear, frustration and pain are the big ones. The desire to escape the clutches of negative emotions like these is what compels people to think or act in a certain way. Maybe your readers are worried about losing their jobs or just want that damn headache to stop.

Of course people are also motivated by love, money, feelings of achievement, recognition and other positives. They work best for ideal readers who have no pains or complaints, who are almost as rare as hen's teeth. For most people, negatives are most likely to spur action.

Don't forget that pain, as the Buddhists see it, does not just come from the emotions or physical body. It is also produced by change, even change for the better. So remember to anticipate and alleviate the pain of any change.

Think carefully about your ideal readers and then pick the deepest fear, frustration or pain. With business communication, the emotions may be more subtle, but they are always there.

Subconscious desires are tricky, but fruitful, terrain. People don't tell you what their subconscious desires are. You have to look beneath the surface.

With most people, subconscious desires are positive yearnings. Dig under the obvious benefit for your ideal reader and you may find the hidden desire.

For example, someone will read your white paper not only for the valuable data, but also to satisfy her subconscious desire to be respected by her peers.

Another will donate to your cause, ostensibly to help the earthquake victims, but more because he wants to feel good about himself. Someone will buy your book on Internet success on the surface to make a fortune, but subconsciously more for the fame or to prove that Dad was wrong.

To touch hearts and be credible, you need to demonstrate that you understand how your readers feel. So select feelings you share. Use an anecdote to explain. For example, a CEO can talk about learning the real truths of customer service when he was a teenager working in fast food.

Short stories are especially effective if you are introducing readers to a new concept they may not fully understand or be comfortable with. By telling a short story, you can persuade them to identify with the hero and open their mind to new ideas.

Anecdotes are one of the best ways to appeal to emotions. In addition to revealing feelings you share with others, you can tell true stories that reinforce your benefits. For example, you can talk about the customer who stopped biting her nails from stress because your software simplified her work. Or you can go on about the sick child who smiled for the first time in months when he met Mickey Mouse, thanks to your reader's donation.

Unless you are a gifted storyteller, you need to keep the anecdote short and to the point, including only the most telling details. No one likes people who tell stories that are too long, in conversation and especially in writing.

Here are my eight tips for writing an effective anecdote:
1. Keep the story very short.
2. Choose your details carefully. You are not painting a picture, but zooming in on the bits that illustrate your point in the most compelling way.
3. Tell stories other people will care about. It's not about you.
4. Don't describe the setting or back story. If it's vital, show it through an action or a revealing detail.
5. State the clear moral or point of your story. Don't assume your readers will get it.
6. Use a conversational tone, almost as if you were sitting around a campfire, all eyes riveted on you.
7. Know your limitations. If you feel that the eyes may be wandering, or worse still, rolling, shorten the story. Remember that a little emotion can go a long way. There's a fine line between schlock and warm and fuzzy.
8. Weave elements of storytelling, such as examples and revealing details, into more of your writing.

Don't forget that few people are great spoken story tellers. Even fewer excel at writing stories. But if you follow these tips, you can succeed with this amazing device.

You'll find more advice on storytelling in the next-level techniques on page 76.

Minds

Although most advice on persuasive writing focuses on emotion, persuaders also need to know how to wield logic. This is especially true if you need to overcome skepticism, as with homeopathic healers, or build trust, as with investment advisers.

So while the heart may be a key sticking point when it comes to persuasion, don't forget to talk to the brain.

You can make your case in two ways:
1. Cite specific cases that lead your reader to a general conclusion, e.g. 90 per cent of the 1,000 people who consumed fewer than 1,200 calories a day for a week lost more than two pounds. So eat less to lose weight.

2. Argue from a generally accepted statement to a specific conclusion, e.g. calorie restriction leads to weight loss, so you should eat less.

Be careful that your evidence and conclusion can bear the weight of close scrutiny. For example, your conclusion about those who ate less may be questioned if some dieters also exercised.

If you are claiming that one thing causes another, make sure you can back that up. Coincidence does not add up to causality. Even if your case is strong, you may be wise to also explain why. For example, with the weight loss argument you could outline the science behind weight loss.

Here, you have to make sure your explanation is clear and accurate. Avoid pseudo-scientific terms such as the tooth whitening ad I read that talked about "powerful oxidizing solutions" that "penetrate the porosities in the rod-like crystal structure of enamel and oxidize interprismatic deposits." What a load of crap.

One of the reasons content marketing is overtaking the hard-sell tactics of the teeth-whitening ad and its ilk is the growing sophistication of consumers. In addition to examples of how your product, service or expertise has helped others, we also want to understand why.

Products like the teeth whitener may sell well at first because saturation lets advertisers find enough stupid or desperate people. But they don't have the strong legs of products and services with claims that can be backed and explained.

There may have been a fool born every minute in P.T. Barnum's time. But with today's sophisticated consumers, social media chatter and the ease of googling suspect claims, people who are in business for the long run are wise to assume that their readers are smart and skeptical.

Inspire

Persuading and inspiring are sometimes considered to be very similar objectives. But here's the difference.

Writing to persuade is based on pointing out specific benefits. It's very individual reader-centered and usually focuses on immediate, concrete rewards. It's all about me.

Writing to inspire transcends the individual, appealing to a large group, a greater cause or higher values. It's all about us.

This distinction explains why U.S. President Barack Obama was so successful at inspiring hope and change, but had difficulty persuading Americans to support many of the specifics of health-care reform.

Inspiration works well with the emotional side of persuasion. Open up your readers' hearts with emotional appeals and stories. Then write about shared values, beliefs and happy endings for all.

To help select the best structure, check out the worksheets on page 92.

You can get a lot of mileage out of the right structure.

6 FIRST IMPRESSIONS

Readers make snap decisions about whether they will open your email, read your report or check out your blog. So you have to hook them right away. In this chapter, I'll explain how to make a first impression that will attract and leave them wanting more.

In the olden days, editors used to write flashy, often sensational headlines. But these days, most people are too busy to be lured in by titillating titles. Because they have so much to choose from, they want help identifying what they want to read, based on specific commitments, not vague promises or cute phrases.

Today, you have to interrupt the endless online conversation so the people you most want to connect with will listen to you. As in conversation, the loudest or most frequent is seldom selected. The star will be the person who grabs attention through interest, emotion, drama or whatever works best for your ideal reader and like-minded people.

Because this is your most valuable real estate, you'll need to invest time here. If you've followed the previous chapter, you will be off to a quick start because you'll know who you most want to connect with, what you want to say and how you're going to say it.

To make a good first impression, the roughly 30 words you devote to your title, subject line or heading and the first paragraph or two should include:

1. a quick summary of what you're going to explain
2. the most relevant details
3. the benefits to the reader
4. a balance of keywords and interest generators
5. an outline of how you're going to explain

1. Summarize

Tell them what you're going to tell them. Chop out any unnecessary verbiage.

No setting the scene, providing background or personal chitchat. Cut to the chase.

Often the most effective opening will inform readers of advice they can immediately apply, such as *5 Ways to Increase Your Email Open Rates*.

Don't make the mistake of those telemarketers you hang up on because they start with a pause or by asking how you are. Get to the point.

Don't start with something everyone already knows, for example the leaves changing color or the stores decorating for Christmas. In this prime space, there's no room for small talk. If you want to warm up your writing with personal comments, save them for your conclusion.

2. The most relevant details

Because so many people stop reading after the first paragraph or two, you have to pack in the vital information up front. Don't wait to tell them what day your meeting will be or whether the kitten will survive.

Think about the five Ws (Who, What, When, Where and Why) and make sure you cover the most important ones as soon as you can. Or zero in on the deep feelings you share.

This creates an inverted pyramid style, where information is presented from the most important to least important. It works any time you think some people will not read through till the end.

3. What's in it for me?

With so much writing clamoring for attention, you need to give readers a clear reason to start and continue by clearly stating reader benefits or emotional connectors in the lead.

Go back to your description of the person you most want to connect with and see how you can max her joy, as in what gets her up in the morning, or ease his pain, as in what keeps him up at night.

4. Keywords and interest

On top of benefits, the title and first paragraph of anything published online have to include keywords. This helps Google and other search engines index your content and also helps searchers find what they're looking for.

Busy people also like titles that clearly identify your subject. Cutesy headlines that provide no information do not work well on the web.

Many newspapers try to compromise, with print headlines tilting toward catchy and online ones toward keywords. Your approach will depend on what you want to accomplish and the medium you're writing in.

So make sure you have your keywords in your title and first paragraph. You score bonus points if you can be catchy too.

To determine your keywords, think about which words or phrases your ideal reader would type into a search box. Or check the terms used to find your website, listing or other ways your ideal reader discovers you. Google and other online tools can help you.

While keywords should guide you, don't be a slave to them. Stuffing your content with keywords annoys Google and other search gods. Besides, you don't want to make keywords more important than your ideal reader.

To show you how ridiculous keyword-inspired titles can be, let me share with you some of the title suggestions I have recently received from Ezinearticles.com. These are based on the keywords people have used to find the articles I post there:

How the Way We Speak Reflects the Way We Write—so stilted

Poetry — Emotions in Writing —but I don't write poetry

Middle School Social Studies Essay Prompts—duh?

Ideally, you need clear titles and first sentences that help people find what they're searching for, combined with teasers, drama, memorable phrases and other ways to reel in readers.

Try to balance clarity with oomph, maybe through a simple title with keywords and a wilder first paragraph. Or a catchy title and a clear first paragraph.

For example, a friend who specializes in creating work spaces that nurture employee innovation is calling the book she's writing *Waking Up the Zombies*. Read a little more and you know it's about bored employees, not the undead. Brilliant.

5. Structure

Your title and lead will also introduce your logical structure. For example, you might be providing five steps to make the most of your LinkedIn profile or telling a story about a dog saving a baby from a cougar.

That's why you need to know how you're going to organize it. This helps your readers and gives you a map to follow for the rest of your writing. It's so much easier than wandering aimlessly. What's more, it's your best guarantee against writer's block.

For example, your title could be:

3 Steps to Sell on Facebook
It's not easy to make money from Facebook, despite what the cowboys claim. They've spent years on target practice.

Alternatively, you could have written:

No Easy Money on Facebook
If you've failed after buying the advice of the easy-money clowns, try following my three proven, targeted steps. They're free.

Writing a great title and lead can be the most thought and time-consuming part of your writing. But by attracting readers and encouraging them to continue, the time is well spent.

It's like spending a little extra time to get ready for a party, a job interview or your first day of kindergarten. You never get a second chance to make a first impression.

Your first 30 words will also help a great deal as you continue writing. Everything you are going to write is already summarized there. So keep referring back if you get stuck.

Chances are your introduction may be longer than 30 words. While it's smart to trim as you much as you can at the outset, don't stop if you can't get it that concise. But remember you'll have more pruning to do later on.

Liven it up

I've separated the section on cramming your relevant information into your lead, a logical left-brain activity, from packing some punch, creative right-brained fun.

That's because you need to not only present the right information, but also make it so compelling that people will keep reading.

Let me stress that there is no way around the need to generate interest through your introduction. Most of us compete for readers' attention many times a day, whether it's an email inviting people to your meeting, a proposal that must stand out from the crowd or your store's newsletter.

If you don't add interest at the start, few people will read you. If you don't continue with interest, fewer will pay attention through to the finish.

Although you've already invested time in your introduction, you need to cough up more. Fortunately, this should be fun.

Because you are writing to encourage interaction, you need to approach it like the start of a conversation with that hotty you want to get to know better.

So let's start with techniques that work in conversation that you can apply to your writing. This will also help you make the transition to the fun side of your brain.

I enjoy talking to people who

- Get to the point
- Use words I understand
- Use colorful expressions
- Consider my interests
- Ask for my opinion, answer or other feedback frequently
- Make lots of references to me
- Mention celebrities, politicians, historic figures and other people we all know
- Tell stories that I can relate to, often funny, exciting or touching ones
- Are easy to follow
- Respect my feelings, values and beliefs
- Provide new or different information and perspectives
- Have clear ideas
- Paint vivid pictures
- Reveal themselves
- Speak with pleasing rhythm and pacing
- Are dramatic
- Aren't afraid to be controversial, argumentative or outrageous
- Inspire

● Make me laugh

Any more you can think of? If you and your ideal reader don't enjoy arguing or would never say anything outrageous, for example, take them off your list.

In addition to adding some of these conversational winners to your first 30 words, keep them in mind when you hit the writing road.

Remember, at this point, no one is reading. Stretch yourself. If you go too far, you can always delete before you send, print or publish.

Otherwise, you will sound like paint drying and wonder why no one seems to have read, understood or acted on what you wrote.

So borrow some techniques from riveting conversationalists and let your imagination run wild.

To draft, revise and practice your introduction, try the worksheet on page 94.

Hook your readers
now or they will
swim away

7 WRITE LIKE YOU TALK

I already explained how most people find writing that sounds like talking is easier and more engaging than the formal approach the teachers drilled into you.

The experts at Flesch, known for their reading comprehension measurement, back me up.

The Flesch human interest test finds much higher interest in content that has lots of personal words and references. What's more, Flesch has proven the effectiveness of conversational techniques such as sentence fragments.

Often people who claim they are conversing on the web don't get this. Too often I read interviews that people have conducted through email or tweets. Or I read prepared statements from politicians and celebrities.

BOR-ing. From their formal stiffness, it's easy to tell the creators jumped from mind to mouse, skipping the natural, social mouth.

I much prefer to interview the people I am writing about in-person or over the telephone. Slogans about customer service or technical terms melt into anecdotes that will grab readers or explanations people can relate to. Sterile descriptions come alive through personality and feeling.

When I type what people have said to me in live conversations, the words shine. The next best thing to live conversation is writing like you talk.

Later I'll give you some tips about the few rules you need to know. For now, I am simply encouraging you to relax.

If you write like you talk, you will intuitively know where to add a comma to indicate a pause or a period for a longer breath.

You won't sound too formal or geeky.

You'll automatically connect your ideas.

You'll ask questions, add emphasis, state opinions and express emotions.

You'll interact with your ideal reader and other like-minded people, not keyboards, screens and your own thoughts. Instead of jumping from mind to mouse, you'll make a refueling stop at your mouth so you'll sound like a human being. Remember to go from mind to mouth to mouse.

How to find your voice

People who write are often advised to "find their voice."

Your voice has been there ever since you uttered "Da-da," as your parents beamed.

Our elementary school teachers insisted that writing is different than talking. True. To go from spoken to written words is an enormous leap. Most of our parents were just as proud when we read our first words as they were when we first spoke.

But many of us were told to abandon what's good about talking when we learned to write. We were taught to be impersonal and objective, to sacrifice opinions and personality to dry analysis and facts. We were prohibited from dangling our prepositions and other organic conversational practices.

Fortunately, many bloggers and other social media people have reclaimed their voices. They write in a relaxed conversational style. They state their opinions. They share glimpses of their personal life. They let us peek inside their heads, much as great novelists do as they develop their characters. They encourage their readers, friends and followers to join the conversation.

Yes, writing relies on more rules and conventions that enable us to understand each other. More thinking is allowed, even required.

But unless your parents "don't got no idea," you already knew most of the important rules before you started to write. That's why, when you're stumped about a rule, your first reaction is to refer back to what sounds right.

Unless you joined a gang or a profession that required you to adopt its dialect, you probably continued to follow the basic language rules you had learned as a kid.

Your voice isn't lost. You use the same voice in conversation all the time, though it has matured with practice, knowledge and emotional growth.

If you want to write in your own voice, imagine that grownup speaking voice and the personality that goes with it. Write.

That goes against much of what was taught in school and reinforced in the work world. So you may need to practice to get comfortable.

Here's how:

1. Shed your conditioning about what writing should be.

2. Practice to gain confidence.

3. Be confident in expressing your opinions, ideas and feelings.

4. Inject enough of your personality, humor and experiences, or the personality of the individual or organization you're writing for, so you won't be mistaken for a robot.

5. Allow yourself to fantasize that you are having a conversation with your partly fictional ideal reader.

Some adults insist that they abandoned imagination along with playing house, war or other childhood games. Trust me;

it's still there, though some people may have to look a little harder.

Writing in your own voice may demand the courage to be controversial rather than going along with the party line.

It can mean being vulnerable, peeling off the formal layers to reveal the person who worries about keeping up with competitors or hates getting dirty.

It can mean injecting humor, providing you are sometimes funny in person.

It can mean throwing in personal tidbits, enough so the people who read you can relate to you as a feeling, reasoning human being.

Remember that old saying: People buy from people not from companies. People are far more likely to participate in your meeting, support your project or buy from you than they are to get behind an impersonal corporate appeal. Be real.

The more your writing sounds like your way of speaking, the more real you will appear to your readers. The more authentic you are, the more likely you are to be trusted and make friends.

If you are writing for someone else, you need to write like an actor who has assumed his character. Your personality and style will likely influence your interpretation.

Similarly, if you're writing for an organization, you are writing as a character you have concocted from brand promises and other materials who probably bears a resemblance to you.

Simple steps

1. Go back to the earlier section on your ideal reader. Review it. Tape that drawing to your screen. Now pretend. It's sort of like how the characters talk to the camera in the television show *The Office*.

Sure, you may not be able to talk out loud from your cubicle. But you can mutter under your breath. With practice, your brain will rewire itself to process writing almost as easily as it handles talking.

2. Paste those first 30 words into your document. You can also add any really important research, though keep it at the end so you can snatch sections as you need them, rather than rely on them too heavily.

3. Don't worry about grammar and punctuation. Go with your gut. Later I'll list the important rules you don't want to break. You can fix them when you revise.

Silence your English teacher censor or that boss who rambles on about synergies and out-of-the-box thinking. Use your own words.

Don't be afraid to use dangling prepositions, sentence fragments and slang.

4. Write as "I" to "you" instead of "we" to "they."

Because you are making a personal connection with the reader, it's better to write as "I," not "we" of the impersonal organization. Remember that you're talking to real people, not categories of clients, shoppers, employees or players. It's a conversation.

Another important reminder: Be consistent. It's confusing to the reader if you switch from, say, "I" to "we."

If you know the person you are writing to, or you're writing to inspire, you can refer to the two or group of you as "we," as long as you're not referring to yourself as the distant royal or editorial "we" that some organizations hide behind. But don't make assumptions if you're in the early courtship-attraction stage.

To imply the interaction of a live conversation, work in hypothetical questions and declarations, for example "Let me tell you… "

5. Follow the examples of good conversation.

What works in conversation works in writing. Review the list from page 33, about what enjoyable conversationalists do.

Your readers speak plain English

You might be comfortable using the technical terms of your profession. But remember you are writing for other people, not yourself. Use plain language, just as you would in conversation with someone who does not share your expertise. This is even more important on the world wide web, where English may not be the first language of many of your readers.

Never, ever try to get around this by providing a glossary. Trust me: No one likes glossaries. Speak in your readers' language instead of trying to teach yours to them.

If you want to attract people searching on the Internet, remember that they are typing in words they understand, not your technical jargon.

Don't try to speak in your ideal reader's dialect unless you are absolutely certain you understand their specialized terms.

For example, a friend was working on a marketing project with a smart young guy whose expertise was in another field.

He sent her an email saying he wanted to explore the customers' "touch points." In marketing parlance, that means the many opportunities to make an impression on a customer. Unfortunately, what he really wanted to learn about were what the customer perceived as benefits.

Think of the money that would have been wasted had my friend not realized the misunderstanding. Think of how bad his well-intentioned effort to fit in could have made him look.

Don't minimize the consequences. The 2008 financial crisis would not have happened if more people understood what was really meant by "collateralized debt obligations" or "credit default swaps."

Besides, like people in conversation, readers are turned off by those who use too many big words. What would have you thought of me if I'd advised you to "eschew obfuscation" instead of "write clearly?"

Talk to your goldfish

By laboring over your introduction, you may have drifted into the formal style of writing you learned in school and polished at work. But if you want to connect with people, you have to lose the tie and jacket in favor of business casual writing.

To warm up your introduction, and prepare for the talking/writing conversation you're going to have next, take your introduction and read it out loud. Although it's best to talk it out with another person, a goldfish will do. As soon as those words have left your mouth, you may realize how stiff your writing sounds.

After you have read your introduction to your colleague or goldfish, revise so it sounds more conversational and engaging.

Then turn away from that computer or turn over that page. Because this part is so short, you'll remember what you have written. Look Goldie in the eyes and speak to her, as if you're striking up a conversation. No peeking at the text.

You may have to do this several times. No problem for Goldie, who has nothing better to do. Keep talking and revising until you can tell she feels the love.

Don't try this with your cat or dog, because they will react to pretty much anything you say. Plus you'll start babbling in that silly baby-talk voice.

Once the conversation is bouncing along, you can continue your writing, resuming the chat with Goldie any time you sense yourself reverting to flat old-school writing.

Although this approach may take longer at first, rehearsing with your goldfish will soon become natural.

8 JUST WRITE

Fasten your seat belt. Turn the ignition key. Switch into drive. Press the accelerator. It's finally time to hit the open road of writing.

Without looking at your notes, pretend you're having a conversation with your ideal reader and start clicking that keyboard. The preparation was valuable, and will be referred to later. But if you write only what you remember, you will capture what is truly important.

Copy your first 30 words. This is your road map, already there, so you can keep your eyes on the writing road. Pedal to the metal.

Write quickly, noting what you need to check or insert later. Do not pause to second guess yourself.

Do not answer the telephone, check emails, listen to music, tweet or do anything else during this enthralling time. Enjoy the drive.

Do not think you can save time by multitasking. Even easy tasks can shatter your concentration. Focus.

If you work in an office, put a "Do not disturb" sign on your door or move to a pod in a silent space. Better still, work from home if you can when you have something important to write. If you are unavoidably interrupted, give yourself a few minutes to regain your focus when you return to your writing.

Do not kid yourself into believing you can concentrate in Starbucks.

Out of this focus, dazzling clarity and energy can emerge. Your mean boss, that nagging ache, the chocolate bar in your drawer, space and time—they will all fade as your focus sharpens.

Don't slow down to fix mistakes. You can do that later. Let it flow.

It's almost as easy as talking. And as much fun as zooming down the open road.

Go!

Finish with a bang

Standard writing advice goes like this: tell them what you're going to tell them, tell them and then tell them what you've told them. Yawn.

What a wasted opportunity to connect with your most important readers, the people who have stuck by you.

You still need to summarize what you've told them, especially how it affects them. But you also need to provide:

1. the call to action, how you want your ideal reader to respond

2. a sense of completion

3. a desire for more

4. a verbal hug or other expression of appreciation

The call to action is often your sales pitch. Do this too early and people won't continue to read. But there's a good chance that people who have made it this far are interested enough to consider buying your product, adopting your point of view or at least continuing the relationship with you.

This call to action needs to be specific and immediate, not subtle. Don't assume your readers will get it.

The action may be symbolic, which will help readers remember. For example, if you want them to care about the environment, you might ask them to write "Reuse and

Recycle" on the back side of a used piece of paper sitting on their desk.

Although immediate actions like this work best, you may also remind them to think about your advice the next time they do something relevant, such as appreciating how the trees clean the air the next time they take a walk.

Instill a sense of completion by reapplying any techniques that hooked readers in your introduction. Think of the circle of life, a problem solved or a case closed.

If you've told a story earlier, return to it and repeat or conclude it.

If you've made a comparison, return, reinforce, rinse and repeat.

Leave your readers wanting more, looking forward to your next post or excited about meeting you. Let them know you're excited too. Don't take this for granted. State it clearly and personally.

Give your readers a verbal hug. That could be the personal comment I told you to defer from your opening.

At the very least, thank them. They took the time to read through what you wrote. Everyone loves to be thanked.

Most readers won't make it to the final paragraph. So don't leave any vital information for the end, unless you are writing a suspense thriller. But do shower the love on the ones who stick with you. They are your most important readers in terms of building sales, visibility or respect.

Like a marathon runner, summon the last of your energy reserves and surge across the finish line. As you hear the crowd cheering, or see the orders rolling in, you'll know that last burst made it all worthwhile.

When I used to write speeches for politicians, I would keep juicing up the big finish until I could hear the audience cheering. Can you?

Take a break

Your brain should be exhausted when you've finished the writing frenzy. Give it a rest. Or at least switch to something different—pay bills, return phone calls, fill out your expense form, read emails, listen to music, hit the gym. Unless I'm on deadline, I don't return to the piece for at least an hour, better still the next day.

Often I try to meditate on nothing.

9 MEMORABLE IMPRESSIONS

You've written feverishly, taken a break and now you're ready to see how you might take your first draft up a notch.

Just as writing was like hitting the open road, this step should be like the return trip, without as many surprise thrills, but a superior overall experience as a result of your 20/20 hindsight.

You'll know to order the largest cosmic smoothie, hike to the tidal flats and take more photos of the people you might not see again.

One of the best ways to up your game is to make it easier for your readers to remember what you've written. After all, there's little point in writing anything, even a quick email, if your reader will forget or have only a faint recall. When you consider how much most people have to read every day, this is no easy feat.

Once you get used to these memory-enhancing techniques, you'll start using them automatically in your first draft. If you've already used some, good for you, but keep reading in case you've forgotten any. We all have memory blips.

Although these techniques are valuable all through your copy, they're especially vital in the title and introduction, which is all many people will thoroughly read, and the conclusion, where your most devoted fans may decide to take the action you suggest.

I'm breaking these memory supplements into vitamins and steroids. I will also return to the basics of memorable conversations, almost everyone's first and favorite way to communicate. And we'll check your draft to ensure you, or the person or organization you're writing for, have left a memorable impression.

Vitamins

These are the same techniques you would use if you were in a grocery store to pick up a few things, but had forgotten your list.

1. repetition
2. clarity, relevance and value
3. concise and precise
4. framework
5. shared experience.

Repetition

The classic memory technique is repetition. With forgotten grocery lists, I automatically ask myself whether we need milk and bananas because they are almost always on the list.

Alliterations are another kind of repetition, as in Reading, Writing and 'Rithmetic. You're much less likely to forget what's on a grocery list that says: diapers, donuts and dairy. Because they are relatively easy to create, however, alliterations can be overused.

Another effective form of repetition is rhyme. Who can forget: "In August 1492, Columbus sailed the ocean blue?"

Or what about the silly rhymes you concoct to remember dry facts when you're studying or to recall addresses? I know I'm not the only one who ends up at that right house because I chant: "6-5-9, feeling fine."

Repetition works well when you summarize in your introduction or conclusion. But too much repetition can be annoying, as we know from all too many TV commercials.

So it's wise to use repetition sparingly and combine it with other memory glues.

Clarity, relevance and value

Your readers' brains prioritize what they're going to hold as a deposit based on its relevance and value. That's why you need to use terminology your readers understand and address their needs and perspectives.

If I had written on my grocery list "a nut of the Juglandaceae family," or "a nut from the tree valued for making veneers," I would not have remembered the walnuts.

Fortunately, I remembered because my kids and I had just been talking about how nutritious walnuts are, which we value.

Even more importantly, as I walked down the grocery aisle, my achy knee reminded me that I had read that walnuts might calm the inflammation. Responding to physical or emotional pain has probably the strongest grip on memory.

Because you have written your first draft for your ideal reader, you should have worked in clarity, relevance and value. But when you're revising, you need to double check or see what more you can do.

Concise and precise

Without a list, I can easily remember three to five items at the grocery store. But the more items I need, the more likely I am to forget.

Readers also have difficulty remembering too much information. So keep it short and focused. No clutter.

Because most of us can remember no more than five items from the forgotten grocery list, five is probably as many points as you can expect your readers to remember. Fewer are better.

Numbers and other frameworks

Numbers help too. If I had known there were five items on the forgotten list, I would have kept thinking until five items were in my grocery cart. While they might not all have been the items on my list, most of them would.

Alternatively, I can remember some of my items by referring to store aisles, a framework, I need to visit.

The structure you chose when you planned will also help your readers remember.

Shared experiences

The grocery list analogy demonstrates how to use a common experience to link the known to the new.

The next time you go to write something that you want people to remember, retrieve some or all of my tips by thinking back to how you remember items at the grocery store when you forget your list.

Bonus tips

First and last : If you've written a grocery list but left it at home, you are most likely to remember the items that were first and last on your list.

Special: If you need to get something out of the ordinary, like a birthday cake, you are more likely to remember it than routine items such as peppermint tea or flour.

Visual cues: work well in grocery stores and writing. When I see the mouth-watering display of apples, I remember they were on my list. Note that I did not have to draw pictures of apples on the actual list

In addition to dramatic visuals that tie into what you're writing, subtle visuals in the type, such as **bolded phrases** or subheads, work too. They encourage your readers to think it's important and tuck it away in their memory.

Steroids

Catchy phrases stick to your readers' brains. Because of that, they can sell gazillions of products, sometimes even change the world. Advertisers spend a fortune creating and testing them.

You too can develop some catchy slogans for your blog, product or cause, by following this advice on creating memory steroids through

1. repetition with a twist
2. visual similes and metaphors
3. compare and contrast
4. the paradox.

I've chosen examples far more memorable than my grocery list prompts and avoided advertising slogans that are so often limited to the shelf life of their campaigns. That's because I want to show you how enduring exceptionally catchy phrases can be.

Repetition, with a twist

The trouble with repetition is that it can get boring. But twist that phrase and you have gold.

Remember these examples?

The only thing we have to fear is fear itself.

Ask not what your country can do for you. Ask what you can do for your country.

Visual similes and metaphors

Super charge words with visual cues plus some elegance and insight and your phrase will be unforgettable.

All that glitters is not gold.

Shakespeare wrote it first, but we still say it today.

Compare and contrast

One small step for man, one giant leap for mankind.

More recently, the Norwegian prime minister Jens Stoltenberg, responding to the Oslo rampage, stated: *Evil can kill a person, but it cannot conquer a people.*

The paradox

Another riveting technique is the paradox, as in *What is the sound of one hand clapping?*

Consider your audience, though, as paradoxes will sail over some people's heads but stick like crazy glue to others.

Unforgettable you

Does your writing sound like you or the person or organization you're writing for?

To check, you may wish to talk to Goldie again.

One reason to write like you talk is to find your own voice or blend it with the personality of the person or organization you're writing for. So while you're revising, look for ways to make that voice unforgettable.

Can you inject some of the personal expressions that your friends love or that are key to the brand? Can you add an anecdote or something else unique to your life or the organization's experience? Does your writing project a distinctive and memorable personality?

While I've encouraged you to be opinionated and fun, please ignore that advice if it's just not you or your company.

If you are the kind of person who plays it safe or you're representing a bank that needs to stress financial safety, that's fine. You won't be as interesting or memorable, but you will be true to yourself. Just don't use this as an excuse to hide.

Any writing beyond your secret diary is social media. Remember that talking is almost everyone's first and favorite way of communicating.

Most of the techniques to aid memory work because they make your writing more interesting, just like colorful friends.

You are unique. Your writing should reflect this.

People do not want to talk to a writing robot. They want to connect with you.

This might be a good time to review the list of conversational techniques from page 33. Or think about the best conversations you've had recently.

To review these memory techniques, see the checklist on page 95.

If you're ready to try to make your writing as memorable as the songs that get stuck in your head, don't miss the final chapter Reach the Next Level.

Readers can't respond if they don't remember

10 FOCUS

When you're writing like you talk, it's easy to go on for too long and to get off track. Now's the time to fine tune.

You'll see how you can make your writing as concise and precise as possible.

You'll reorganize words and phrases, moving them to where they belong, eliminating redundancies and becoming easier to follow.

In addition to the details, you'll look at the big picture of what you have written to make sure it accomplishes the objectives you set earlier. You'll also widen your lens to include other important people.

Shorten

In order to respect your busy readers' time, you probably need to shorten dramatically. Losing the fat will also let them see your buff writing muscles and your main point.

This doesn't apply only to Twitter and other social media with character limits. It applies to anything for busy people.

In fact, I recently read about a top military officer who insists that every report must fit on a single index card. I salute you, sir.

If you started out with a clear idea of what you wanted to say, you may have limited the excess. But no doubt you'll find more to chop at this point.

Here's my advice:

1. Copy your draft document. This way you can chop aggressively with no worries. Once you have made your document as short as possible, you can select any specifics that need to go back in. You'll probably be surprised by how little there is.

2. Start with individual words that are redundant. For example, why write "free complimentary" webinar when "free" and "complimentary" mean the same thing?

3. Look for words that have snuck in from your corporate or technical jargon. Nuke them.

4. Examine your adjectives and adverbs. Are they necessary? Do they help readers understand what you're saying? Reduce, refine or remove.

5. Take aim at fuzzy expressions. Often several unclear words or phrases can be replaced by one precise term.

6. Pretend you are being charged money for each word you write. Hack out some more.

7. Search your document for the word "that." You need this word more when you're talking than when you write. You may be amazed at how much you can reduce your word count this simple way.

8. Replace longer descriptions with links for the relatively few people who want more information.

When I first started working at a daily newspaper, my feelings were hurt when my editor told me to chop my article in half. But the result was so much better. In fact, over the years I've found cutting my length in half is usually wise advice.

People often feel possessive about what they've written. But if you want to connect through writing, don't let your ego get in the way. Remember it's not about you. It's about keeping your busy readers happy and hooked.

It's about writing better. And showing off those buff ideas.

Here's an example of how I would have shortened a page from a government web site. This sounds like it was written by a committee or went through multiple approvals, where everyone felt pressure to "add value," as they say.

Skim through to get the basic idea or you'll risk falling asleep and missing the finely diced rewrite that's more than 75 per cent shorter.

Before: 390 words

Ontario is on the move again. This is an exciting and demanding time in the history of our province. We need to grow stronger in a more competitive world and we have a plan to get there.

This past year, Ontario launched a five-year Open Ontario Plan to strengthen our economy and create more jobs. Growing our economy means being open to change, opportunities and our new world. In this report, you'll read more about that plan and what it means for Ontario families.

Working together we've made a lot of progress over the past seven years. In our schools the number of students in Grades 3 and 6 meeting the provincial standard is up 14 percentage points and graduation rates have risen from 68 to 79 per cent. We've made room for 200,000 students in our colleges, universities and apprenticeship programs.

In health care, wait times are lower — we've gone from the worst in Canada to first. We've created more nursing positions, and over one million more people now have a family doctor.

Since the global economic recession struck, things have been difficult for many Ontario families. We lost 250,000 jobs. Many of us know someone who was laid off, perhaps even in our own homes. Yet, we've already gained back 76 per cent of the jobs we lost.

Since May 2009, we've created more than 188,900 net new jobs. Retail sales are up 5.5 per cent, from this time last year. Manufacturing sales are up nearly 14 per cent and exports are up 15 per cent. We've gone from being one of the Canadian provinces hit hardest by the recession to one of the fastest growing. And we did it by working together.

This is the seventh in a series of progress reports that have been issued by the Ontario government. But they're really about what Ontarians have accomplished by working and building together.

We've come a long way — but there's more to do. And we have a plan to keep Ontario moving forward.

Weathering the global recession: How Ontario prepared ...

Job Creation Stimulus
Training
Improvements at Employment Ontario
Research and Innovation

A Post-Recession Economy: Open Ontario

Training Ontarians for the future
Protecting Health Care
Ontario's Future Jobs
Tax Plan for Jobs and Growth
Action for the North
Farming and Rural
Fiscally Responsible Government
In Your Community

After: 86 words

The five-year Open Ontario Plan is pulling us out of the recession. So far, we have:

- Created nearly 190,000 new jobs. More about job creation
- Sent 200,000 more students to colleges, universities and apprenticeship programs. More about training
- Increased exports by 15 per cent. More about economic growth

Read our progress report to learn more about
Employment Ontario
Research and Innovation
Health Care
Future Jobs
Tax Plan for Jobs and Growth
Action for the North
Farming and Rural
Fiscally Responsible Government
Your Community

How did I do it?

I zeroed in on the key message: Ontario is recovering from the recession.

I focused on a few numbers to back that claim, rather than confusing readers with lots of statistics they wouldn't remember.

I integrated key information with links, giving readers choice on which item they wanted to pursue in detail.

I deleted all the editorializing, positioning and other words that could be replaced by "Ya-da-ya-da-ya-da." For example, what did they mean by "Ontario is on the move?" Earthquakes? Union with the U.S. Democratic states?

Of course I may have missed a couple points important to the committee or the ideal reader. Once the length has been reduced, it's easy to pick exactly what needs to be added back in.

Never forget that people are busy. They want the basic facts and easy opportunities to explore specific areas in greater detail.

For a checklist on how to shorten your content, go to page 96.

Reorganize

Another way to reduce the length is to make sure your writing is well-organized. This will also intensify your focus.

In the heat of writing, phrases often slip in where they don't best belong. So move or delete them.

Modifiers work best right beside the word they modify, e.g. "The book costs **only $25**," not "The book **only** costs **$25**."

If you're not certain where a word or idea fits, cut and paste it at the end or on another document. As you continue to revise, you may find the perfect spot for it. Or you may find it's simply not required.

If you have trouble organizing, create another document. Write your most important subheadings and paste all your related ideas under them. Your ideas will become more logical and you'll likely find you can delete some repeats.

By grouping everything together, you may discover logical connections that enable you to simplify your subheads or reduce the number of main items on a list.

Once you are clear on your organizational structure, you can add more subheads or other techniques to help your readers navigate.

After you've reorganized, you need to read through again and add connecting words or phrases to make sure your ideas flow.

Try the worksheet on page 97.

Review your plan

Now's the time to **review your worksheet on your ideal reader, starting page 88**. Will your ideal reader, and like-minded people, understand you?

Has your image of your ideal reader evolved or changed as you have written? If so, do you need to revise to reflect that?

Have you touched your ideal reader emotionally or on a subconscious level, for example the desire to look good in front of others?

Will your ideal reader have read, remembered and be primed to respond to what you have written?

Will your ideal reader be likely to think, feel or act the way you want? Can you do more?

Review your worksheet on your point, page 91.

Does your main point come across clearly?

Have you stated it in the introduction, expanded on it in the body and linked it to a call to action in the conclusion?

Can you compose a tweet or other short summary based on your main point?

Review your worksheet on structure, starting page 92.

Did your structure succeed in accomplishing its objective? For example, did you leave your readers with steps they can follow and refer back to? Or did you inspire them?

If not, go back and see what you need to do. Don't feel bad if you need to rewrite here. It's like taking your return trip on the much better route you discovered.

Does what you have written make sense? Are there holes you need to fill or details you need to add? Is there proof you need to provide?

Widen your lens

Earlier I advised you to concentrate on your ideal reader to nurture intimacy. When you're revising, you need to broaden your focus to encompass all the other people who will be reading what you've written. This includes the people who may be editing or approving as well as those who may be deciding your raise, promotion and other career prospects. Maybe your Mom or old sweetheart too.

That means using words that a wider range of people will understand, another point scored for plain language. It may mean adding context or details to make sure everyone gets what you're talking about. What's more, it probably means going beyond the motivations and benefits of your ideal reader.

Take a look at the worksheet on page 98.

If a baby boomer, older person or someone educated in snooty English or colonial schools or other grammar stickler is approving your copy, you will need to get pickier about your grammar and punctuation.

One of my respected colleagues cannot bring herself to utter the grammatically imperfect title of this book. She calls it: *Write **As** You Talk*. True story.

Make sure
others don't
feel left out

11 FIX

I know that you, my ideal reader, don't enjoy all this fussing. But if you gloss over this part, you may leave mistakes that smudge your sheen.

This chapter will also spare you the embarrassment of hitting send, print or publish, only to realize you've missed a typo or left yourself open to misunderstanding.

Think of this stage as the dental floss of writing hygiene. With practice, it will become an easy habit. And you'll be ready to move to the next level, far cheaper and more fun than cosmetic dentistry.

I will cover only what you absolutely need to know. Those who are more interested in following the rules should consult the style manuals and visit the many sites devoted to the fine points of grammar.

It's not that I don't like rules. In fact, I belong to a LinkedIn group whose members spent months passionately debating the need for serial commas (apples, oranges and pears versus apples, oranges, and pears).

But I've come to the conclusion that there are bigger fish to fry. In my many years of editing and reading, I keep coming across the same mistakes. I'm not upset about breaking rules, especially those that no longer help. But let me insist on the rules that help us to understand each other.

I also hold dear a few that can make your writing more intimate and friendly.

Fortunately you, my ideal reader, are not a grammar purist. But you want to avoid the fumbles that can confuse your readers and make you look like an amateur.

If you need to please a fundamentalist or if you are a word nerd, consult Grammar Girl, Grammar.net or similar web sites. Those who want to concentrate on the important rules only can learn pretty much everything you need here.

Because of past trends in the education system, many people missed out on learning the rules. Others seemed to have forgotten what they were taught, just like I have no clue about calculus.

So don't feel bad if you need a refresher. Read on and I'll tell you the big ones you need to know. I have provided only five rules for grammar and a simple minimalist punctuation philosophy. If you keep checking back with these few rules as you write for the next while, you'll soon start applying them without thinking.

The easiest and most common way to know what's correct is to ask yourself what sounds right. If you were raised by reasonably articulate English-speaking people, you will understand intuitively. But there are exceptions you need to know.

I'm not trivializing grammar rules. In fact, I'm so intent on eliminating the most dangerous offenses that I'm calling the next section the war on bad grammar.

Ka-boom!

The war on bad grammar

Despite the many books and sites devoted to grammar, we still see the same serious issues, everywhere from executive memos to television news crawl to school report cards.

Most of these problems persist because they can't be caught by spell check. Some are caused by confusion over important distinctions between spoken and written English. Others come from people who try too hard.

1. Confusing possessives with contractions

We learned in school to use an apostrophe to demonstrate that something belongs to someone, as in "the girl's homework." Sadly, many people forget the vital exception to this rule with the pronouns "it," "you" and "they." Here, we skip the apostrophes on possessives, reserving it to indicate that we have combined, or contracted, the pronoun and verb, as we do often in conversation and less formal writing:

Its (possessive) and it's

Your (possessive) and you're

Their (possessive) and they're

Ask yourself if you could instead say "it is," "you are" or "they are." If you could, then add the apostrophe. If not, leave it out.

Or recite this simple rhyme:

> *It's*, **apostrophe, means it is**
>
> *Its* **is possessive, just like his**

Finally, there is no such word as "its'." Ever.

2. Other sound-alikes

People who rely on spell check too much often mix up words that sound the same but are spelled differently because they have different meanings. If you want your readers to understand and think you're smart, you must choose the right one.

Consider the difference between writing "I accept your proposal," and "I except your proposal." I'm sure you don't want to confuse your readers this way.

Although there are way too many to list here, here are
some of the most common ones:

accept	except	
affect	effect	
alternate	alternative	
boarder	border	
cite	site	sight
complement	compliment	
chord	cord	cored
council	counsel	
coarse	course	
discreet	discrete	
elicit	illicit	
epic	epoch	
farther	further	
founder	flounder	
gasp	grasp	
heard	herd	
insight	incite	
peak	peek	pique
pedal	peddle	
principal	principle	
right	write	
reign	rein	
storey	story	
than	then	
verses	versus	

If you want to stop embarrassing yourself and confusing
your readers, write a list of words you have mixed up and
display it prominently in your work space. If you are the

slightest bit confused about any of the words on this list, start with them.

When you have a smidgen of doubt, check that you're using the correct word by highlighting it and clicking on spelling & grammar or research in Word or the equivalents on other word processing programs. It takes only a few seconds, much less time than we used to spend hauling the fat dictionary off the shelf and leafing through.

Once you've caught yourself a few times, using the correct one will become automatic. Then you can cross it off the list. As long as you haven't had to add too many new ones, you will feel good.

You may not be aware of these slip-ups. So when a sound-alike mix-up is pointed out to you, usually by a baby boomer or anal person, don't be defensive. Thank them. Add the words to your list.

3. Me, myself and I

I don't enjoy seeing the hornet's nest stirred when word nerds debate pronouns. As long as people understand, I just don't care about the technicalities.

What does get me going, however, is the "me," "myself" and "I" debate. That's because the misuse can make people sound pretentious and impersonal.

As children, most of us were taught to avoid saying "Me and David went to school." But somehow many of us ended up thinking there's something terribly evil and self-centered with "me," even when it's correct.

Fortunately, the right way is easy to remember. The same goes for "myself," which is usually fumbled by people who are still trying to please the nuns or other childhood ghosts.

So go back to what sounds right when you talk. And remember these two easy tips:

1. Use "I" in the subject of the sentence only. So "David and I walked to school" is correct, but "The dog followed David and I" is not.

2. Use "myself" only when referring to something you did, as in "I did it myself."

4. That, which, who

If you can't decide whether to use "that" or "which," ask yourself if you could be saying which one. Or just think of which witch is which.

Use "who" instead of "that" when you are writing about a person, as in "Tiffany, the girl who sits beside me." The use of "that" with a person is dehumanizing.

5. He/she/it/they

The trouble often occurs when people want to avoid being sexist or employing the awkward "he or she" construction. Here's a simple rule, which purists don't agree with. If your reader will understand, you can use "they" when you're referring to a singular general subject, such as the team, the client or the user.

Here's an example: "The team won the award because they are so good at customer service." Although "team" is singular, your readers know that the term refers to more than one person.

However, if you are writing for grammar sticklers, you might want to turn "team" into a plural by referring to "the team members" so you can correctly use "they" on the next reference, as in, "The team members won the award because they are so good at customer service."

Or, if you're giving hypothetical examples in longer content, you can alternate between "he" and "she," as I've done in much of this book.

To fix these common errors, consult the checklist on page 99.

Minimalist punctuation

Just as grammar rules need to serve the purpose of helping us understand and connect, so do punctuation marks. The biggest mistake people make is to use too much punctuation.

Fancy punctuation marks, especially apostrophes, are often abused. So I recommend reducing those risks by following my philosophy of minimalist punctuation.

The basic rule is: If your punctuation mark will help your readers understand, use it. If not, don't bother. When you're in doubt, read your sentence out loud and decide whether commas or other marks would help.

Minimalist punctuation is not only easy to follow, but will also keep your content looking clean and uncluttered.

If you use a style manual to determine your punctuation and similar issues, remember to apply its rules consistently. Here in Canada, most of us use the *Canadian Press Stylebook*. In the U.S., it's the *American Press Style Guide*. Most book publishers rely on the *Chicago Manual of Style*. Large organizations often publish their own guides.

Commas

Lynne Truss explained commas well in her best seller *Eats, Shoots & Leaves*. Her title demonstrates their vital role. If you write "The panda eats shoots and leaves," your reader can easily understand that you are referring to the animal's food. If you add the comma and write "The panda eats, shoots and leaves," the reader is left wondering what the panda shot before he left.

Commas are also helpful when you have a set of words that belong together. For example, "Pandas, who live in China, eat bamboo."

Without the commas, you might have concluded that only pandas who live in China eat bamboo, not all pandas. The comma clarified this.

The serial comma has no place in minimalist punctuation. Although style books differ, followers of minimalist punctuation write apples, peaches (no comma) and pears. That's because the word "and" is doing the job of a comma. The comma is unnecessary.

So think twice before you use commas. Remove unnecessary ones when you're revising your work.

Busy-body-boomers approving your work may re-insert the serial or Oxford comma. Challenge them. If they say they are following the Canadian or American Press style guide, they should not add this superfluous mark.

Quotation marks

While you need to use quotation marks when directly quoting what somebody said or content from another source, competent writers should not rely on them often to distinguish an unusual spin on words. To make sure readers will get you, not "get" you, try removing the quotation marks.

If I thought you needed the quotation marks around "get" to get me, I would have looked for a clearer word.

As a last resort, you can use quotation marks to help your ideal reader understand an unusual use of a word, but do this too often and you'll look like an amateur.

Semi-colons

You can use semi-colons as super commas to separate items in a list that already has commas (Granny Moses, chief executive officer; Jed Clampett, chief operating officer; Jethro Bodine, chief financial officer).

You can also use semi-colons to link two related thoughts (MySpace is dead; Facebook rules).

But that's it. Don't use them to string together too many thoughts. Stop. Start a new sentence instead. The shorter the sentence, the easier it is to understand.

Exclamation points

Nothing says hack louder than too many exclamation points. Like swear words, exclamation points are best avoided or reserved for very special occasions when they can help you deliver a strong, dramatic message.

Apostrophes

A few pages ago, I explained how often people confuse apostrophes on contractions and possessives. Don't forget this. It's probably the most important piece of punctuation advice you'll ever receive.

If you are going to be a minimalist punctuator, you will also avoid using apostrophes to denote plural numbers or letters, as in hits of the 1980s or mind your Ps and Qs. You understood me without the apostrophes, right?

Avoiding apostrophes with these kinds of plurals will also prevent you from using them mistakenly with other plurals. I know this is common sense, but who hasn't recently seen a sign that says something like "Banana's on special?"

The more often you allow apostrophes in plurals to creep in, the wider you are opening the door to apostrophe abuse.

To review your punctuation, use the checklist on page 100.

Other style issues

Capitalization

When it comes to capitals, my preference is for lower case on everything but proper names as well as the first word of titles and sentences. That comes partly from my long-time reliance on the Canadian Press Stylebook, but also the fact the lower case words are easier to read and look less pretentious.

On the other hand, titles in blogs and websites usually capitalize all the main words.

From experience, I know it's a slippery slope. Article titles are one thing. But once people start to capitalize job titles and departments, they are soon capitalizing words like Synergy and Share-Worthy, just to give their words a God-like status, or should I say god-like.

Capital letters do not help readers grasp the significance of a term. In fact, they can scare them. DON'T OR ELSE. See what I mean?

If you want to inject gravitas, a better approach would be to clearly explain what you mean and how it affects the reader. Strategic concepts, such as Paradigm Shift and Onboarding, may be important to leaders, but capitalizing could make these concepts look pretentious rather than important.

If you do capitalize, for example job titles, remember to switch to lower case when they no longer resemble a proper name. Take the examples of "Director, IT" but "The directors attended the meeting," or "googling suspect claims."

Lengths of sentences, paragraphs

If you have ever put your copy through the Flesch test or other readability measurement, you know that short sentences and paragraphs are easier to understand.

Because people's eyes focus on the left side of the screen, it's even more important to use short sentences and paragraphs for anything that will be read on a computer.

If you have a compelling reason to use a long sentence, go for it, but follow it with short sentences, fragments or questions. Got that?

Numbers

If you're using numbers, you may also need to check with a style guide and consistently apply rules for writing dates, times, numerals versus written numbers, seriously large numbers and different currencies.

Most style guides advise you to write out numbers under 10, as in three and four.

However, you can break these rules if you have a good reason and do it consistently. For example, I often use numerals in titles because they take less space and stand out.

When you're writing a report or anything else that involves lots of numbers, you need to make them relevant to your reader. Unless you require precise long numbers for statistical veracity or other sound reasons, round them off or express them as simple fractions. To qualify them, use adjectives like "roughly," "an estimated," "approximately," "around," "about," "more than" or "fewer than." For example, "33 per cent" could become "more than 30 per cent" or, better still, "about one third."

Remember that numbers on their own can be meaningless. You need to relate them to something relevant to the reader. For example, you can compare sales figures to equivalent numbers for another time period, possibly illustrating this with charts and graphs.

Visual metaphors work especially well for ideal readers who do not enjoy numbers. For example, telling people that the snow on a typical Aspen chalet roof weighs as much as two baby elephants is far more likely to get them shoveling than saying the roof is covered with roughly 400 pounds (182 kilos) of snow.

Metaphors work even better when they relate to your ideal reader's specific interests. If she's a football fan, you could illustrate the large number of people visiting your site by comparing it to the number of football stadiums they would fill.

Stating how many times something would stretch around the world is a metaphor that is used so often it has become a cliché. Plus, you can't see it. Try to be memorable by coming up with an original metaphor your ideal reader can visualize and appreciate.

Choices

You'll find the answers to many style questions in the style guides I referred to earlier. If you write for other people, you'll need to follow their favorite guide or recommend one.

Sometimes you have choices. For example, even though I am Canadian, I am using American-style spelling for words like color (not colour) and center (not centre) because I think the leaner U.S. spelling is easier for people to follow, especially international audiences. Besides, my ideal reader is American. I have tried to ensure no Canadian spelling slips in, though it's difficult to break long-standing habits.

The necessary pain of proofreading

Let me start by admitting I am proofreading-challenged. I expect people will find typos in this book.

My brain switch flips off when I'm supposed to be proofing my own writing. I gloss over those little mistakes that can make me look unprofessional.

I also have trouble paying the strict attention that proofing other people's writing demands.

Contrary to what many people appear to assume, spell check does not eliminate the need to proofread. It sucks people into a false sentence (oops, I meant sense) of complacency. It lures them into the trap of confusing the word they intended with a similar-sounding, correctly spelled word.

No matter how sophisticated word-processing programs become, they won't catch that you've written "star" when you meant "start" or "form" instead of "from."

Even if you are a poor proofreader, there is hope. Let me share the strategies I use to compensate for my proofreading disability.

1. Have a picky person read your content.
2. Print out your copy.
3. Look for common confusions.
4. Review more than once.

1. Have a picky person read it

It's best not to rely solely on friends or blog buddies, especially if you're working on a big important assignment. Hire a professional or find a picky person in your office, preferably someone who enjoys pointing out your errors. Every office has one.

My teen daughter often proofreads my writing, not simply because she's good at it and always needs money, but also because she loves pointing out my mistakes.

If you're more comfortable in the creative right side of your brain, you urgently need the balance of a logical, left-brained person. Let them know their corrections are welcomed. Do not be defensive.

Everyone needs to proofread. Most of us need an objective, fussy proofreader.

Don't assume you can't afford a professional. Most are quite a bargain.

Tell your proofreader what your consistent style is. For example, be specific about when you use upper case in titles. Refer him to the style manual you use. Make sure your proofreader checks your links.

Review what your proofreader has caught. This will help you learn. Besides, even professional proofers overlook the small stuff sometimes. Don't be too smug, as many of them can be sensitive about even the smallest miss.

If you're detail oriented, your writing may contain fewer flaws. But you probably still gloss over minor glitches. You may also need an editor to take a big-picture look and tell you if everything hangs together. In fact, anyone who needs more help should hire a qualified editor.

2. Print out your copy

I will copy content from software that doesn't let me print and paste it into Word just so I can proof this way. This advice is especially important if you choose not to use a proofreader.

It's the best way to catch tiny preposition flubs such as a missing "or" or confusing "of" or "on."

Printing gives you a much-needed change in perspective from reading on the screen. Often I proofread in a different room or outside, when the weather is nice and the neighbors aren't using chain saws.

Better still, print then read out loud.

When you find a mistake, use the search and replace function to avoid repeat goofs.

For extreme proofreading, grab your buddy and read each word out loud, back and forth, from the end to the beginning. Yes, backward so your mind can't automatically correct.

3. Look for common confusions

The most common mistakes involve confusing "It's" (contraction of it is) and "its" (possessive), "you're" and "your" and "they're" and "their."

Also, be on the lookout for missing prepositions, articles and other wee bits that are easy to skip.

4. Review more than once

You may want to focus on a particular aspect each time, such as sound-alike words or links. If you can, take a break between each round.

Remind yourself of these pesky details on the checklist on page 101.

After the fact

One of the best things about writing for the web is the ability to fix mistakes. Some people enjoy alerting you to them. So thank them and get on it right away.

Don't resend an email or reprint a piece unless the mistake is toxic. You don't want to draw attention to mistakes that most readers will miss anyways.

Proofreading misses may not only make you look stupid, but can also make your writing more difficult to understand. So take them seriously.

While our tolerance for typos and other mistakes has risen with the frequency of email and tweets, don't forget that more people writing makes for a more competitive world. If you want to stand out and look like a professional, make your writing as goof-free as you can.

12 REACH THE NEXT LEVEL

You have read this book and practiced with the worksheets and checklists.

You have planned what you want to say and how you're going to say it. You have thought about who you most want to connect with.

You have written like you talk while having an imaginary conversation with your ideal reader.

You have checked over your writing to make sure you have accomplished your objectives, been concise and precise. You have added some techniques to help your readers remember. You have fixed the flubs that could have made you look less intelligent that you are.

But you know you could do better. You have to do better if you want to stand out and connect with more people.

You want to be able to look in the mirror and say: "This is my best yet."

How do you take your writing up a level? How can you make a connection so deep that your ideal reader and like-minded people will respond?

Let's look at how movies, music and other media do it. Even if you don't aspire that high, you can dramatically improve by borrowing the techniques of the masters.

Stories

Why stories? Because stories are social, memorable, mind-opening and behavior-changing.

This is a hard, cold fact confirmed by neuroscientists, including Jonah Lehrer in his book *How We Decide*.

You are more likely to be riveted by a story than a lecture or fact sheet. Compare the impact of a university history textbook to the historic fiction of novels, television series and movies.

No wonder the best conversations start with "What's new?" and continue with a story.

Stories work best when we can identify with the hero. Take the children's classic *The Three Bears*. It wasn't popular when the original protagonist was a snoopy old lady. But when rewritten as a tale about innocent Goldilocks, parents cared and children identified.

Stories open minds, the first step to changing behavior. Recently I read *The Happiness Project*. Had author Gretchen Rubin simply given me a list of things to do, I might have brushed off the book as more fluffy self-help. Instead, she told me the story of her happiness project. I read through the book in a few days and immediately started boosting my happiness, by playing the piano and resuming other activities I had assumed I was too busy to do.

Stories are also behind the profound behavior changes of Alcoholics Anonymous and other 12-step programs. People decide to make difficult changes not because of beatings, films about reefer madness, their doctor's lecture or free pills from the pharmaceutical representative. They summon the courage to make difficult changes because they can relate to the feelings, fears and experiences of people telling true stories at the meetings.

The same goes for raising money. Statistics, no matter how startling, may not persuade me to donate to the Somali famine victims. But tell me the story of a starving mother trudging hundreds of miles with her frail children and I'm whipping out my credit card.

With employee communication, stories work too. Tell the story of what one employee did to cut costs or win a customer service award and you have provided an example for others to emulate. This is much more effective than a cranky list of things to stop or start doing.

And what could be more persuasive than a case study that tells the story of how you solved someone's problem?

When I talked about how to structure your writing to achieve results, I discussed anecdotes, concise stories that may consist of only a quick example or a passing personal reference. Stories are better, but demand far more skill and the willingness to reveal vulnerabilities.

One of the mistakes I see practical writers make is to confuse a chronology with a story. "This happened, then this, then this," they write, wondering why no one is responding, even though they've read that stories are such an excellent way to move people.

They have failed to base their story on a conflict that will drive the plot. Sometimes people don't like to admit they have a problem. But how can you have a solution, let alone a story, unless they have a problem?

In addition to your main conflict, you may need a series of obstacles that build the conflict and suspense.

Take the example of a story about a new operating system. The system needs to be fixed or replaced or enhanced because it's not working fast enough, easily enough, cheaply enough or whatever. That is the central conflict.

As the system is developed, there will be misunderstandings about business requirements and technical capabilities. Obstacles. Problems will be revealed during tests. More obstacles.

Users will get frustrated adapting to the new system. Problems, problems.

Add to that the way Murphy's law seems to plague big projects and you can see that this kind of story has a wealth of problems and obstacles. But you need to be open and honest about them.

Stories also need a hero, real and likeable for readers to identify with, and a villain, to drive the plot.

You can get away with hypothetical characters in quick examples, but with practical writing, your heroes should be real. The intelligent people you want to appeal to can smell fake heroes a mile away.

The hero of the story is not usually someone high in the org charts or the world. We want stories about people we can identify with. When we see that a product worked for someone just like us, we are tempted to give it a try. When we hear heroic stories about people with sick pets and bills and problems like us, we are encouraged to try better the next time we are faced with a similar challenge.

If you are the hero, try to be humble through self-deprecating humor or confessing to a weakness your readers share. Don't boast, much as I refrain from mentioning my many beauty pageant tiaras when I tell my story. Just kidding.

Although it's vital for your ideal reader to identify with your hero, don't forget the rest of the gang. If the boss tells a story about his golf game to non-golfers or about his kids to child-free employees, their eyes may glaze over. But if he tells golf stories to golfers and kid stories to parents, they are sure to engage and get the point. He can broaden the appeal by talking about competitive pursuits other than golfing or people outside his family who depend on them, though that will dilute the impact of his story.

Like problems, villains are often difficult for some practical writers to portray. Although you may be able to pin the blame on a ruthless competitor or the fat cats on Wall Street, chances are you won't have a Voldemort or Darth Vader.

You may have to set up an inanimate villain, such as a natural disaster, economic crisis or flawed DNA. The drama will be weakened, but not drained, as long as you have a negative force to power the plot.

With practical writing, stories usually have a clear point, which is directly linked to what you want your readers to do. The resolution of the conflict will prove your point. Clever storytellers will delay the point till the conclusion, much like the punch line to a joke.

In the wrong hands, this can backfire. If the point doesn't quickly become obvious, your readers may feel like you do when you're listening to the sales rep drone on, while you drum your fingers and say to yourself: "Get to the point!"

When you start your story, you don't have time to fully describe the setting or explain the context. To grab attention, lead with the central conflict. To engage your readers, relate it to them.

For example, you could start a story about how you climbed out of debt by writing "You know what it's like when you go to the bank machine and it won't give you any money to buy groceries for your kids?"

After this, you can go back to quickly explain what led up to this conflict, then how you resolved it and how your readers can too.

Although you want to keep your stories real, you can minimize details that would bog down the story or humiliate your heroes. For example, I will often tighten dialogue or clean up glaring grammar mistakes, especially if the hero's first language is not English. I don't need to mention that my hero has a wandering left eye or wacky jewelry, unless those details are vital to developing the character or plot.

I don't go too far cleaning up my characters because they have to be credible. Even television commercials where the people are obviously played by actors work better if they seem real—and just like me.

If you want to learn more about storytelling, read the great novelists and how-to books. Think about what draws you into your favorite movies. Pay attention to how short stories are told in television commercials. Deconstruct how a friend told you an entertaining story about his weekend calamity.

And keep in my mind these five storytelling tips:

1. Lead with the central conflict, to draw in your audience.

2. Immediately introduce a hero who people can identify with.

3. Describe only details that will develop your character or plot. Whenever you can, demonstrate details through actions rather than descriptions.

4. Have the hero surmount obstacles on the way to resolving the conflict.

5. Set up your point through your story and hammer it in the conclusion.

I am focusing on the practical writing that you do more and more of every day. And I'm insisting that your stories be concise.

Your ideal reader is busy and you are not Chaucer or Stephen King. But if you learn to tell true stories based on conflict and resolution, you could be far more successful at involving your audience and making your point.

For a checklist on storytelling, see page 102.

Borrow from Hollywood

Another way to take your writing to the next level is to borrow the Hollywood magic of sex, romance or humor. Because of the risks, many people won't try. But if you are the kind of person who communicates through innuendo, flirting or laughs, go for it. Done well, the benefits are enormous.

Sex on the sly

I am not suggesting you start telling dirty stories or making sexist comments. But you can often spice up your writing through subtle sexual references. Remember the legendary Clairol hair coloring ad slogan: "Does she or doesn't she?"

Or what about the recent Old Spice television campaign with the hunk in the towel?

If you go too far, you will turn off your ideal reader and alienate your boss. But even in the most conservative setting, you may be able to hint by calling your new software or cupcake recipe "hot."

Or you could write about cheating on your smartphone by hooking up with another company's Wi-Fi. Or compare looking for customers to cruising the singles bar.

Love me, love me

Although fulsome romance may be too much for the kind of writing you do, remember the longing for personal fulfillment almost everyone feels. Engagement is all about people feeling connected and valued. Sounds a lot like romance to me.

That's why you need to keep the focus on the reader and use friendly language, as you would in an intimate conversation. You can't hold a reader at an objective distance and expect them to feel you care.

As in real life, that means more than saying how much you value your customers, employees or other special people. You have to show the love by describing what you've done for others (stories again) or offering an award, special deal or other display of affection.

Laugh dammit

If you are funny in person, take a shot.

Laughter is one of the best ways to hold readers' attention and drive home your message. You remember the presenter who got you laughing, but not the dry expert. You changed behavior because of a movie that opened your mind with laughter, then delivered a punch.

Yet many people think anything work-related needs to be serious. They worry that a joke could offend, inspire ridicule or make them look unworthy of promotion.

Because it's not backed up by body language and tone of voice, it's easier for written humor to be misconstrued.

But, handled the right way, the risks are outweighed by the rewards of happier readers who are far more likely to read, remember and react to what you have written.

To make sure your readers understand you are joking, you might need to add a quick explanation, such as "Just kidding," "LOL" or "☺." Your choice will depend on what works with your ideal reader and feels comfortable to you.

Stay away from sarcasm and any humor that could take a nasty turn. If you're in doubt about your use of humor, ask someone who will be brutally honest.

Funny stories often work well on their own or pumped up with exaggeration. Be yourself with self-deprecation, observational humor, satire, fantasy or silliness. But don't get too carried away or you won't sound real.

Use the kind of humor that works for you. If you're not good at telling jokes, don't even try. If you are known for wise cracks, let loose.

The point is to cultivate your personal brand of humor. As Jerry Seinfeld said: "The whole object of comedy is to be yourself and the closer you get to that, the funnier you will be."

Think of the kind of standup comedian you could be, then try to write that way. Or not.

The magic of music

You know what it's like to have a song stuck in your head? What if you could create those kinds of ear worms with your writing? People would be unable to stop thinking about you.

Okay, perhaps that's a little exaggerated, but I think it's worth taking a closer look. Let's see how this ultimate stickiness works and how you can apply it to more mundane communication.

A while back, I read a book by musician-turned-neuroscientist Daniel Levitin called *This is Your Brain on*

Music. I am fascinated by what scientists are learning about the brain and how it affects how we think, feel and act.

I learned that the songs that get stuck usually have a hook that grabs us, emotions that hold us and rhythm that gets us moving.

Hooks grab us

The hook has to be simple enough to easily grasp but not so simple it blends into the background. This hook repeats, varies and returns.

Repetition is, of course, the classic memory-enhancing technique. On its own, repetition becomes dull, dull, dull. But repetition becomes supercharged when the theme varies.

Consider *Beethoven's Fifth,* possibly the stickiest piece of classical music ever. It starts with the hook: "Da-da-da-DA. Da-da-da-DUM."

This hook repeats, then varies in note and rhythm. After branching into some new themes, the orchestra returns to the hook.

My hook is *Write like you talk—only better.* As well as repeating it, I have examined it from different angles. But I keep returning to the sociability of talking and the thinking of writing. Okay, I'm no Beethoven but I'm trying.

Do you have a hook for what you're writing?

Emotions hold us

A great example of the emotional resonance of sticky songs is Adele's *Someone Like You,* last summer's achy-breaky international hit. It was number one around our house because my daughter sings it so well.

Few things are sadder than a breakup when you're around the age of Adele or my daughter. And even though it's been many years since my heart has been broken, I can remember the pain. I'll bet you can too.

Although heartbreak may not be the emotional hook you need, consider whether you can tap another deep emotional pain of your ideal reader. For example, I am more likely to buy from tech people who know how my shoulders clench when the new gadget doesn't work the way it's supposed to than from those who expect me to relate to rainbows and holding hands with people around the world.

Rhythm moves us

Think about people spontaneously playing air guitar to rock songs or pretending to conduct a symphony orchestra. What a reaction.

Though perhaps not this extreme, you might get a better response by paying more attention to the rhythm and other sounds of your writing.

Written words lack much of the auditory gusto of music. But not all.

Think of the novelist whose rhythm embraces you so tightly you can't put down the book. Think of how you just heard Beethoven and Adele in your head.

Think of words like squish, swoosh and thump. Think of how sound bites live on in written words.

Try to incorporate some sound-like elements into your writing. Now click those ruby slippers three times and you'll be back in Kansas. Tap. Tap. Tap. Whoosh!

This connection with sound is also behind my insistence that people write like they talk. Just like we replay songs in our heads, there's something mesmerizing about hearing voices. Even if they're all in our heads.

Mindful media

Paying attention to what works in movies, music and other media will yield lots of insight into how to better communicate and connect.

It's often said that good writers must be avid readers. Not necessarily. Although most professional writers love to read, we also have to soak up and analyze other media.

So don't worry about feigning a reading passion. Read what you enjoy. Reverse engineer the media that works for you. Understand the form of expression that's loved by your ideal reader.

I've learned more about storytelling from television than I have from great literature because the formulas are simple and tested.

From programs like *Law and Order*. I know that you need to open stories with the murder, or central conflict.

From commercials, I've confirmed that you should deliver your pitch only after you've solved the problem.

You need to be especially mindful of what works for your ideal reader.

For example, if you're an accountant, don't limit yourself to *The Wall Street Journal*. Immerse yourself in what's enjoyed by the person you most want to connect with and like-minded people—maybe hockey, opera, artisanal cheese magazines, video games or crazy pet photos.

You've probably heard people insist that Facebook games, Google+ or other shiny new things are what everyone should focus on. If your ideal reader is plugged into one of these passions, this makes sense. But you may find the person you most want to connect with is scarfing down some other slice of our increasingly niched media world.

You can't savor every media and interest. But you can focus on what grabs you and your ideal reader. Instead of passively absorbing, you can take the time to think about how it works.

When a song gets stuck in your head, think about how that happened. When you read a classic like *The Adventures of Huckleberry Finn*, listen to how Mark Twain speaks in Huck's voice. When a sound bite from a politician's speech flies around the world, dissect it. When a commercial persuades you to buy something new, ask yourself how it succeeded.

It all starts with conversation

While media niches may differ, almost everyone loves to talk. That's why my approach is based on what works in conversation. Think about the conversations that prompted you to make new friends, lived on in your memory or opened your mind to something new.

Talking is our first and favorite way to communicate. That's why what works in live conversation influences all other media. Two people talking is the original social media. Everything else is but a pale comparison.

Like conversation, social media, email and other forms of computer-enabled collaboration are interactive. Unlike live conversations, they are usually written. If you communicate through them, it's vital to write like you talk.

The more these written conversations sound like live ones, the more likely they are to result in the same kind of deep connections that conversations build.

If you write with the intimacy of a one-on-one conversation, you will connect. What's more, you will attract more people who share your interests and passions. As more people connect, you will create a community.

If you write like you talk, you will harness the social dynamics of conversation. If you write better than you talk, you can super-size your chatter with the thinking of the written word.

That's all you have to do to get closer to living your dream. Good luck.

13 WORKSHEETS AND CHECKLISTS

To get the most out of this book, practice what you need to improve. Next time you are writing something important, fill out the worksheets that will benefit you most. Keep doing them until they become automatic.

    If you'd like to use electronic worksheets, go to http://www.stickycommunication.ca/book/worksheets.

WORKSHEET: Your ideal reader
From page 12
If you'd like to use electronic worksheets, go to
http://www.stickycommunication.ca/book/worksheets-2/.

Who is your ideal reader?
Age
Gender
Education
Income
Profession
Interests
Values
Pains I can relieve
Problems I can solve
Passions I can tap into
Joys I can increase
Words my ideal reader would use
Words I use that my ideal reader would not understand

How do you want your ideal reader to
Feel?
Think?
Act?

What works best with your ideal reader?
Emotion
Logic
Facts
Fun

Shock
Other
All or some of the above

What subconscious motives drive your ideal reader?

What gets her up in the morning?

What keeps him awake at night?

WORKSHEET: Your personality

From page 14
If you'd like to use electronic worksheets, go to
http://www.stickycommunication.ca/book/worksheets-
2/.

What's your personality?

How will you convey it?

OR
What's the personality of the person or organization you're writing for?

How will you convey that?

What gets her up in the morning?

What keeps him up at night?

WORKSHEET: What is your point?

From page 17
If you'd like to use electronic worksheets, go to
http://www.stickycommunication.ca/book/worksheets-2/.

Step 1
In as few words as possible, write the main point you
want your reader to get and remember.
Step 2
Shorten. Eliminate unnecessary words. Reorganize words
so you can cover more than one thought under the same
umbrella of words.
Step 3
Connect your main point to your ideal reader and
objectives.

Here's an example.
Draft 1, 29 words
To further the patient's journey, a holistic range of
treatment modalities will be directed towards positive
outcomes for a complex array of co-morbidities, including
ambulation deficits and psychiatric impairments.
Draft 2, 15 words
To help the patient, various treatments will be applied to
different physical and mental health problems.
Draft 3, 21 words
You won't need to worry when your parent returns home,
because we'll have investigated and treated probable
health problems.

WORKSHEET: Which structure?

From page 19
If you'd like to use electronic worksheets, go to
http://www.stickycommunication.ca/book/worksheets-2/.

Select the best structure to achieve your objectives.

Inform
What subheads or other organizational frameworks will you use?

Instruct
What do readers need before they can begin?
What are the steps they must follow?
What should the result be?
What else can you use to help, e.g. illustrations, video links?

Advise
What are your three most important tips?

Persuade, hearts
What are the emotions you need to plug into?
Which pains can you relieve?
What problems can you solve?
Do you have a compelling story?

Persuade, minds

Are you arguing from a general rule to a specific outcome?

Are you arguing from a specific outcome to a general rule?

Can you establish a causal connection?

How do you back up your claims?

Inspire

What noble aspirations do we share?

How can we help the world?

Multiple structures

If you are combining more than one structure, how are you doing it?

WORKSHEET: Lively leads

From page 28
If you'd like to use electronic worksheets, go to
http://www.stickycommunication.ca/book/worksheets-
2/.

Write your title and first paragraph, using as many drafts
as you need to reach that sweet spot of information and
interest.
Copy them.
Now revise them to create a more interesting,
memorable conversation.
Don't worry about what your boss, your prospect or your
high school English teacher would think. Don't run away
from thoughts you'd be embarrassed to say out loud. This
is for your eyes only.
Read it out loud to your goldfish or a very patient
colleague. Keep revising and talking until you feel you
have struck up a conversation.
Write your conclusion. Have you:
Summarized
Offered a sense of completion
Reinforced the benefits
Provided a specific call to action
Left them wanting more?

CHECKLIST: Memory

From page 46
If you'd like to use electronic worksheets, go to
http://www.stickycommunication.ca/book/worksheets-2/.

Can you aid your readers' memory in any of these ways?
Repeating your main point, but not too often
Alliterations
Rhymes
A message that's clear, relevant, valuable to the reader
A narrow focus, with fewer than five things to remember, ideally only one
Organizing the information by numbers, problem-solution, geographic regions, chronological order or other framework
Visuals that will prompt the reader to remember later on
Subheads, bolded text and other type visuals
Experiences or feelings that you and your ideal reader shares
Catchy phrases
Similes, metaphors or analogies
Comparisons and contrasts
First or last on a short list
Special or extraordinary
Repetition with a twist
Capitalizing on what's memorable about you
Questions, commands and other conversational techniques

CHECKLIST: Shorten

From page 53

If you'd like to use electronic worksheets, go to http://www.stickycommunication.ca/book/worksheets-2/.

1. Have you deleted all redundant or otherwise unnecessary words?

2. Have you changed or deleted any words specific to your world that your readers might not understand?

3. Have you replaced fuzzy phrases with precise words?

4. Have you eliminated as many "that"s as you can?

5. By how much have you reduced your word count?

6. Can you shorten some more?

WORKSHEET: Reorganize

From page 58

If you'd like to use electronic worksheets, go to http://www.stickycommunication.ca/book/worksheets-2/.

Are your adjectives and adverbs beside the words they're supposed to modify?

Are your ideas together or helter-skelter?

Paste all your sentences and phrases that aren't in the perfect spot at the bottom of your document.

Write logical subheads, idea buckets. Paste sentences that belong in them. Does this sharpen your clarity? If so, revise accordingly.

WORKSHEET: Other readers

From page 60
If you'd like to use electronic worksheets, go to
http://www.stickycommunication.ca/book/worksheets-
2/.

In addition to your ideal reader, who else will be reading
what you've written?

Have you included their motivations and benefits?

Have you used terms they will understand?

Have you provided enough context and other information
to ensure they get you?

Should you follow grammar and punctuation rules or
other concerns that matter deeply to them?

CHECKLIST: Grammar

From page 62
If you'd like to use electronic worksheets, go to
http://www.stickycommunication.ca/book/worksheets-2/.

1. Confusing possessives with contractions
Did you use "its" as a possessive and "it's" for "it is?"
Did you use "your" as a possessive and "you're" for "you are?"
Did you use "their" as a possessive and "they're"
 for "they are?"
2. Other sound-alikes
Is there a tiny possibility that you could have confused other words that sound similar? Check the list on page 64.
3. Me, myself and I
Were you correct, as in
x and I took a walk
He went to the store with me and x.
I did it myself?
4. That, which, who
Did you refer to things as "that" and people as "who?"
Did you use "which" only when you meant "which one" or in the sense of "which witch is which?"
5. He/she/it/they
Did you use "they" to refer to a singular subject because your readers aren't fussy about grammar? Or did you change the subject to a plural or alternate "he" or "she" because they are grammar sticklers?

CHECKLIST: Minimalist punctuation

From page 66
If you'd like to use electronic worksheets, go to
http://www.stickycommunication.ca/book/worksheets-2/.

1. Is each of your commas helpful to readers? Have you left out any that could help them?

2. Can you get rid of quotation marks around words that aren't direct quotes and still have the reader understand you? If not, is there another word or phrase you can substitute?

3. Have you used semi-colons only as super commas or to link two short thoughts? Can you replace some semi-colons with commas or start a new sentence instead?

4. Is each and every exclamation point really necessary? If you can use an exclamation point only once, where's the best place?

5. Have you used apostrophes correctly with possessives and contractions? Can you eliminate apostrophes used with numbers, letters or other plurals?

6. Does your page look cluttered by punctuation?

7. Will all your punctuation marks help your ideal reader understand?

CHECKLIST: Pesky details

From page 69
If you'd like to use electronic worksheets, go to
http://www.stickycommunication.ca/book/worksheets-2/.

Have you applied capital letters consistently?

Have you over-capitalized?

Have you written as "I" to "you?"

Have you rounded off numbers?

Have you provided context for your numbers and used metaphors that mean something to your ideal reader?

Are your sentences and paragraphs as short as can be?

Is most of your copy aligned to the left of the screen?

Have you used a picky proofreader? If not, have you taken the time to print, read aloud and check thoroughly?

CHECKLIST: Storytelling

From page 76
If you'd like to use electronic worksheets, go to
http://www.stickycommunication.ca/book/worksheets-
2/.

Does your story open with a conflict and hero your ideal
reader can relate to?

Does it set up, build and deliver your point?

Could your story be shorter without losing impact?

Is it believable?

Is it based on conflict, problems and obstacles?

Can your readers unite against your villain or at least
relate to enough conflict to move the story along?

Have you selected the best details to develop the
characters, advance the plot and make your point?

Have you made your point clearly and compellingly?

ABOUT BARB SAWYERS

Let me explain how this blend of talking, socializing writing and thinking came together for me.

I talked early—and often—as my family and friends would all tell you. I wrote early too, tales of princesses and castles in chicken-scratch printing.

Then in grade three, I drew lines under some words and brackets around others. I understood the mechanics of language intuitively, as if I possessed mysterious knowledge passed on from the ancestors.

This gave me a way to compete with my younger brother, the smartest kid in the school, county, possibly the country. Like Brian—or Brain as we called him—I could get perfect scores in English grammar and later in French and German.

In university, I gave up on foreign languages when I realized how tedious and lonely the labs were, parlaying with an eight-track tape recorder.

Also in first year, my history prof loved my debut essay because I analyzed instead of just listing the chronology. As my new major, however, I chose philosophy because it gave me more time for socializing. And it sharpened my thinking.

But I got tired of sliding into hot pants in order to earn a living as a cocktail waitress. I still loved writing. So I took a graduate degree in journalism.

I ended up in corporate communication. I was thrilled to be at the center of the action, advising executives and politicians on what to say and helping employees, customers and other people make sense of their rapidly changing world.

Well before social media let us *Comment, Like* or *Follow*, I knew that writing to persuade people to respond in a certain way was ultimately a social activity. Crafting speeches and scripts confirmed the power of writing like you talk. Why didn't other people get it?

Just when I thought I'd scream if I got stranded on one more iceberg of a memo along came the bloggers and other social media people. Many wrote like they talked. They called it a conversation. Finally I could combine my love of talking, writing, grammar, socializing and thinking. I had found my tribe.

Many of the social media people needed me too. To sound smarter and be easier to understand, they needed to know the five grammar rules that still matter. They needed to know where to temper the spontaneity with planning.

My flame reignited, I wrote my book, first as posts on my blog, www.stickycommunication.ca/blog, and later as an ebook I sold on my site.

I gave presentations and taught workshops based on my philosophy of combining the sociability of talking with the thinking of writing. I listened to what readers and other people had to say. I thought. I read. I rewrote the book.

Here I am, one step closer to fulfilling my potential. I hope you are too.

To continue the conversation, you can contact me at barb@barbsawyers.ca or comment and connect with me and other readers at my site at http://www.stickycommunication.ca/reader-community/.

WRITE LIKE YOU TALK—ONLY BETTER

10498531R00065

Made in the USA
Charleston, SC
09 December 2011